Noteworthy

LISTENING AND NOTETAKING SKILLS

PHYLLIS L. LIM
University of Arizona

WILLIAM SMALZER
Fulbright English Teacher Training Program
Cairo, Egypt

NEWBURY HOUSE PUBLISHERS
A division of HarperCollins*Publishers*

Director: Laurie E. Likoff
Production Coordinator: Cynthia Funkhouser
Text Design Adaptation and Cover Design: Suzanne Bennett Associates
Text Illustrations: Blaise Zito Associates
Compositor: Bi-Comp, Incorporated
Printer and Binder: Malloy Lithographing, Inc.

Chapter opener photo/illustration credits

Chapters 1, 7, 9, 11, 13: Skjold Photographs. Chapter 2: *Open Doors 1985/86,* courtesy Institute of International Education. Chapter 3: Official U.S. Immigration and Naturalization Service Photograph. Washington, D.C. Chapters 8, 16: Catholic News Service. Chapter 10: Ron Meduescek/Arizona Daily Star. Chapter 12: University of Arizona. Chapter 14: courtesy New York Stock Exchange. Chapter 15: UPI/Bettman Newsphotos. Chapter 17: *The Arizona Judiciary,* Arizona Supreme Court, Administrative Office of the Courts. Chapter 18: courtesy Washington, D.C., Convention and Visitors Association.

NEWBURY HOUSE PUBLISHERS
A division of HarperCollins*Publishers*

Language Science
Language Teaching
Language Learning

Noteworthy: Listening and Notetaking Skills

Library of Congress Cataloging in Publication Data

Lim, Phyllis L.
Noteworthy : listening and notetaking skills / Phyllis L. Lim, William Smalzer.
p. cm.
ISBN 0-06-632637-0
1. English language—Textbooks for foreign speakers.
2. Listening. 3. Note-taking. I. Smalzer, William, 1946–
II. Title.
PE1628.L48 1990
428.3′4—dc20

89-13352
CIP

90 9 8 7 6 5 4 3 2

Preface

Noteworthy is a high-intermediate to advanced level ESL/EFL laboratory textbook with three major goals:

1. to improve listening comprehension and develop academic notetaking skills through extensive practice
2. to provide foreign students with a deeper, clearer understanding of life and culture in the United States
3. to increase oral proficiency by providing opportunities for students to respond to the input they listen to and take notes on

Learning new vocabulary is an important part of each lesson, and several important notetaking skills are presented and practiced. However, overall we have used a content approach. The final activity of each unit is a written quiz covering the content of the three lectures in the unit. The quizzes, which are found at the end of the book, are perforated and can be easily pulled out.

The topics of the 18 scripted lectures are generally universal and academic in nature: climate, geography, population, economics, law, and agriculture, for example. The vocabulary is mostly subtechnical, found and used across disciplines and in different professions. There is a general progression from easy to more difficult within each unit and from the beginning to the end of the book. The lectures are delivered in a relaxed, natural speech style.

An effort is made to help students see the organization of a lecture in English, to see both the forest and the trees. Motivation to take good notes is built in, as students need their notes for oral activities soon after the lecture and for a quiz some time later.

In addition to Cassettes, a Teacher's Manual containing answer keys and tapescripts, as well as a comprehensive quiz, is available to aid the teacher.

We wish to thank students at the Center for English as a Second Language at the University of Arizona as well as Katie Allen for their kind help in testing these materials.

To the Teacher

Teachers will find that *Noteworthy* offers versatility. The text has three purposes, any of which can be utilized in any given situation. The first purpose is to provide listening and notetaking practice, the second is to provide information about the United States, and the third is to provide the subtechnical vocabulary that will be useful across disciplines if the student later attends an English-medium university, particularly in the United States. A teacher who chooses not to devote the extra time needed for students to take notes could still use the materials for listening comprehension with a focus on cultural content. Individual lessons could be used to provide background information for further treatment of a topic. And, of course, the teacher who wishes to concentrate on oral production could use the lectures as input for the accompanying oral exercises. Provided below is an explanation of the purpose of each segment of a full lesson, which requires about three 50-minute periods to complete if each segment is done.

Note: The symbol 🎧 in the margin indicates that the material needed to complete the listening activity is on the cassette that accompanies the text. The symbol ↻ indicates that it will be necessary to rewind the cassette to the beginning of the exercise or lecture for a second or third listening of the same material.

Chapter Outline

Illustration: to introduce the topic, to stimulate students' curiosity, and to begin establishing a cognitive schema for the lecture

Predictions: to have the students make an investment by predicting the content of the lecture through their questions. As students share their prediction questions with the class, a schema for the content is further established.

Vocabulary and Key Concepts: to familiarize students with new subtechnical vocabulary and with the major concepts of the lesson

Notetaking Skills: to give students strategies for saving information in an organized manner and in a meaningful, usable form

Listening: to lead students through a series of listenings to distinguish the main subtopics from supporting details. Some guidance is given, but content is stressed over skills, and the emphasis is on repeated practice at notetaking, especially in the first ten lessons.

Accuracy Check: to check students' comprehension and the completeness of their notes, generally by means of a ten-question objective quiz

Oral Practice: to provide oral activities in pairs or small groups or as a class which use the content of the lecture as input to improve students' oral competence. At the same time, students check the completeness of their notes, which they use for these activities.

Review: reconstruction of different portions of the lecture

Transfer: generally, questions for discussion treating a similar topic in the students' countries or questions which expand on the content of the lecture

Homework: to provide a final look at the key vocabulary of the lesson or an expansion of an important concept from the lecture

Follow-ups: to make sure the students are on the right track and to allow students and teachers to evaluate their progress in the lesson

Unit Quiz: to provide students an opportunity to use their notes to take a quiz over one, two, or three of the chapters of a unit. Quizzes require either short answers or more extended answers, some of which require synthesis of material.

Suggestions for Teaching and Approximate Time Required for Each Activity

Illustration and Prediction Questions: Ask students to use the title and illustration to brainstorm about the topic and write three questions they believe will be answered in the lecture. Students may work individually, in pairs, or in small groups, or this activity may be done at home. After students share questions as a class, you may wish to ask them to discuss these and one or two additional questions from the Answer Key (depending on the questions they generate or do not generate themselves). These questions are designed to tap students' previous knowledge on the topic and to alert students to the main ideas of the lecture. Depending on the level, background, and amount of support your students need, you may wish to vary this activity by giving them the "suggested/possible questions" from the Answer Key to discuss, instead of writing prediction questions. These questions will point them more directly to the main ideas of the lecture. *Time:* up to 10–12 minutes if all done in class.

Vocabulary and Key Concepts: Have students quickly read through the sentences silently before they listen to the dictated sentences on the tape. You may also ask them to do this prereading as homework along with the previous activity. After they listen to the tape and fill in the blanks, quickly go over the spelling of each word and discuss the meanings of any word or words they ask about. *Time:* up to 10–12 minutes if all done in class.

Notetaking Skills: Go over the skill and have students practice the skill if appropriate. Try to move quickly, as they will practice the skill again in the lesson. Some notetaking skills exercises could also be assigned as homework, and those that are prelecture readings should be, if possible. *Time:* will vary depending on the skill being practiced and whether it is done in class or at home.

Listening: The first ten lessons call for three listenings for each lecture and an optional listening outside class for those students who fail to get at least 70% correct on the Accuracy Check. Subsequent lessons call for two listenings and an optional third listening. There is nothing magical in these numbers. More advanced students may do well with two listenings from the beginning. Try to limit whole class listenings to the general level of the class. Try to maintain some pressure without reaching the frustration level. If possible, provide an opportunity for slower students to listen additional times *outside* class. Ideally, in one class period you should get through at least the Prelistening Activities and the First Listening. *Time:* depends on length of each lecture and number of listenings done in class.

Accuracy Check: Do as quickly as is feasible. After students listen to and answer questions, discuss only answers students do not agree on. Try to raise their consciousness about why they missed an answer. Did they misunderstand the lecture or the question? Was the information missing from their notes? Was the information inaccurate? Or were they unable to *locate* the information in their notes? Sometimes students are trying to write down too much and missing relevant information, or they may simply be unable to locate information they have in their notes because they fail to see the organization of their notes. Ideally, the Accuracy Check should be completed and gone over by the end of the second class. *Time:* up to 10 minutes.

Oral Practice:

Review: Be sure every student is involved in the review by having individual students responsible for assigned sections of the lecture. You can vary the activity by having students work in pairs or in small groups. Students can deliver their part of the lecture to a partner or small groups or, from time to time, to the whole class. You may wish to skip this part of the lesson depending on the goals of your course if time is short and students seem satisfied that their notes are complete enough for the follow-up quiz. *Time:* 10–20 minutes depending on complexity and length of lecture.

Transfer: Pair work is probably ideal, especially if you can pair students from different countries. Small groups may also work well. Give students a time limit for discussion in pairs or groups and assign one person to report for the group when appropriate. While not essential to the lesson, transfer activities should help to maintain student interest and involvement in the lessons. Ideally, the oral practice should be completed during the third class hour. (If time permits, you may wish to have students do or begin the homework in class or begin the prelistening activities for the next lesson. Many homework activities lend themselves to pair or group work.) *Time:* will vary greatly depending on activity.

Follow-up: Keep the follow-up activities as brief as possible. Besides providing feedback, they are also meant to remind students of the purpose of the just-completed activity in some cases and to provide closure before moving to the next activity. *Time:* 2–3 minutes.

Homework: Assign to be done inside or outside class. (See *Transfer.*) These assignments are not essential to the lessons and may be omitted as desired. Put answers on the board and discuss only those answers students disagree on. *Time:* will vary greatly depending on the activities and whether done in class or not.

Unit Quiz: Because the unit quizzes can be used in a variety of ways, they merit a somewhat longer discussion. The primary purpose of the quizzes is to provide motivation to take good notes and to simulate a university experience. In a university class students take notes which they later use to study from to prepare for tests. The time interval can be rather short, or it can be quite long—several weeks, for example. Our ideal use for these quizzes would be for the student to take one for all the chapters in a unit at the end of each unit. However, you may not want or be able to complete all the chapters in a unit. In that case, it would be possible to use the part of the quiz which deals with whichever chapter or chapters have been completed. If you decide to use the quizzes for two or three chapters in the unit, we suggest that you pick and choose from among the questions of the two or three quizzes depending on how much time the students will be allowed for the quiz and the level of the students. We further suggest that you assign point values to the individual questions chosen to add up to 100 points and let the students know how much each question is worth. Of course, the point values should reflect the difficulty level of the question in your opinion. In general, detail questions should be valued less than questions which require the students to synthesize knowledge. You will, of course, need to indicate to the students the particular questions that you have selected for them to answer and the point value you have assigned to each of the selected items. This could be accomplished most simply by writing the numbers of the selected quiz items and their point values on the blackboard. An alternate method would be to circle the numbers of the selected items and to write the point value of each of these items on the quiz papers themselves.

Teachers can decide whether they wish their students to study their notes outside class or whether they wish to allow their students to use their notes while taking the quiz. Students should understand that they are expected to write complete sentences for those questions which are starred (*).

Some teachers may prefer to give quizzes at the end of each chapter. In that case, they may simply use the appropriate part of the quiz for that chapter. *Time:* up to one class period depending on how many chapters are being covered and how many questions are being asked.

Note: While the chapters in each unit are related to a common theme, they do not in general depend upon each other, and it is not necessary to do the first chapter in order to do the second or third chapter. However, for the unit "The Face of the Land" we do suggest that the chapters be covered in sequence or at least that the first chapter, on geography, be covered before either the chapter on climate or the one on agriculture.

Contents

To the Student

You can use *Noteworthy* in two different ways depending on your purpose for learning English. If you wish only to learn what makes the United States different from your country or wish to learn about the country before visiting it, the content of the lectures will be useful and interesting. If you are preparing to study at a university in the United States, or in an English-medium university elsewhere, the notetaking skills you will learn by practicing will be essential in your academic career. The content of the lectures will also give you a better cultural understanding of the United States, that will make your studies easier and provide a richer experience should you visit the United States.

The Table of Contents shows you *what* you will learn about the United States. Below is a list of notetaking skills you will become more proficient in:

1. using abbreviations, key words, and correct number notation to save time
2. recognizing relevant information in order to focus on the essential information in a lecture
3. structuring your notes to make them more understandable and usable
4. following the lecturer's rhetorical cues and hints to know where he or she is going
5. preparing for a lecture by reading
6. using visual aids such as maps to help you follow a lecture

Conscientious use of *Noteworthy* will give you a larger vocabulary, better comprehension of spoken English, an ability to take notes effectively, an improved ability to speak in English about a variety of topics, and last but not least, a deeper, clearer understanding of another country and its people.

UNIT I

The Face of the People

1. Population
2. Foreign Student Population
3. Immigration: Past and Present

CHAPTER 1

Population

1. Prelistening Activities

A. PREDICTIONS

Using the title of the lesson and the illustration as a starting point, share with your classmates what you already know or think about this topic. Then write three questions you think will be answered in this lecture.

1. ______________________________

2. ______________________________

3. ______________________________

Follow-up: After you have written your questions, share your questions with your teacher and your classmates.

B. VOCABULARY AND KEY CONCEPTS

You will need to understand certain vocabulary words in order to follow the lecture on population. You will also need to include some of these words in your notes. Before you listen to the lecture the first time, you will have an opportunity to try to write these words as you hear them in sentences. You will then have a chance to check your spelling and comprehension of these words.

Directions: Write the word or words you hear in the blanks provided in each sentence. For example, you will see: Most countries take a ____________ every ten years or so in order to count the people and to know where they are living. You will hear: Most countries take a *census* every ten years or so in order to count the people and to know where they are living. You will write the word *census* in the blank. Do your best to spell the missing word or words correctly.

1. Most countries take a ____________ every ten years or so in order to count the people and to know where they are living.

2. A country with a growing population is a country which is becoming more ____________ .

3. A person's ____________ is partly determined by skin color and type of hair as well as other physical characteristics.

4. The majority of the U.S. population is of European ____________ .

5. The ____________ ____________ of a country gives us information about where the people are living.

6. Black people ____________ ____________ over 50% of the population of some American cities.

7. The total population of the United States ____________ ____________ ____________ many different kinds of people.

8. A city whose population increases but whose area stays the same becomes more ____________ ____________ . That is, there are more people per unit of space.

9. The average age of the population of the United States has been getting ____________ higher over the last several decades.

10. The use of antibiotics has greatly decreased the death rate throughout much of the world.

11. A country whose birth rate is higher than its death rate will have an increasing population.

12. On the average women have a longer life span than men do.
(期間, 一生)

Follow-up: Check the spelling of the dictated words with your teacher. Discuss the meanings of these words and any other unfamiliar words in the sentences.

C. NOTETAKING SKILLS

Abbreviating

During today's talk you will need to write down the names of several geographical areas. To save time you should use abbreviations. You can abbreviate in any way you like. We have written a few examples of abbreviations for you. Remember that you can develop your own system of abbreviation for notetaking. What *is* important is to try to abbreviate to save time during notetaking and to use abbreviations that *you* can remember. Now write your own abbreviations for the rest of the geographical names below.

California	Cal.
Florida	Fla.
East Coast	E. Cst.
Eastern Seaboard	E. Sb
Midwest	Mid W.
South Central	S. Cen.
Gulf of Mexico	G. of Mex.
West Coast	W. Cst.
Illinois	Ill.
Ohio	Oh.
Michigan	Mich.
New Jersey	N.J.
New York	N.Y.
North Carolina	N.Ca.

Pennsylvania	Penn.
Texas	Tx.
People's Republic of China	PROC
Soviet Union	VSSR
India	Ind.

Follow-up: Now that you have finished writing your own abbreviations, cover the left column with a piece of paper and use your abbreviations to recall the place names. If you can recall the place names from your abbreviations, you are successful.

Using Visual Aids

You will also need to know the names and locations of some large geographical areas of the United States. Take a minute to look at the map of the United States before the lecture begins to familiarize yourself with these areas.

2. Listening

A. FIRST LISTENING

Listen for general ideas. After a brief introduction, the lecturer lists his three subtopics. He then goes on to discuss each one individually. As you listen, write down the three major subtopics in the spaces labeled ST 1, ST 2, and ST 3 below.

LECTURE

NOTES

Introduction: Governner Census

1. PROC most populous country
2. Ind. Second "
3. VSSR third "
4. USA fourth " – 241 million

ST 1. Race and origin – 241 million

White 79%
Black 10%
Hispanic 6%
Others 5% (Oriental & native)

ST 2. Geographical destribution (where people live)

5 of most densely population → E. Sb.
(NY, Penn, NJ, N.Ca. Fl.)

Most populated of W. Cst. → Cal.
" Sou Cap. G. of Mex → Tex. (3rd)
" Mid. W (Central) → Ill., Oh., Mich.

ST 3. Age and Sex (1980 89. census)

95 million men for each 100 million women
95 – 100.
12m more women.
The average is 31.5 years old.
life span
higher death rate
increasing (dec bir late
Thcer life span
more male

Follow-up: Now check your major subtopics with your teacher.

B. SECOND LISTENING

While listening again, write down as many relevant details as possible below the main subtopic with which they belong. Remember to abbreviate where possible to save time.

LECTURE

Follow-up: Check your notes. Do you see places where you think you missed important information? If you had difficulty getting the important information, you may not be using enough abbreviations. This is a good time to check to see if the lecturer answered your questions.

C. THIRD LISTENING

This time try to complete your notes while checking the ones you already have. Look at your notes before the lecture begins to see where you might have missing information.

LECTURE

Follow-up: Keeping in mind that you will use your notes for a comprehensive quiz later on, compare your notes with your teacher's or your classmates'. Do you need to listen to the lecture again?

3. Postlistening Activities

A. ACCURACY CHECK

Listen to the following questions and write short answers. For example, you will hear: What was the population of the United States according to the 1980 census? You will write: 241,000,000 people. You may use your notes. You will hear each question one time only.

1. USSR
2. Black
3. 6%
4. E. Sb.
5. Cal.
6. Mid W.
7. 950000
8. Male
9. Increasing (slowly)
10. 3% 5

Follow-up: Check your answers with your teacher. If you had less than 70% correct, you should listen to the lecture again and check the accuracy and completeness of your notes.

B. ORAL PRACTICE

B.1. Review: Working in pairs, use your notes to practice giving sections of the lecture to each other. Student A will present the introduction and subtopic 1 and its details to Student B. Student B will present subtopics 2 and 3 and their details to Student A. Following his or her own notes, the student who is listening should check the accuracy and completeness of his or her partner's presentation.

Follow-up: Were your notes complete and accurate enough for you to do this oral practice activity with relative ease? Did you and your partner agree on essential information? If not, you may need to listen to the lecture again.

B.2. Transfer: Prepare a short report about the population in your country. Use an encyclopedia or an almanac to help you. Take brief notes. Do not copy sentences. Tell your class the size of the population and where it is distributed geographically as much as you can determine from your research or from your personal knowledge. Tell what are the most populous regions or cities. Tell the class about the race or origin of the population in your country also. Is the population in your country increasing or decreasing? Why?

C. HOMEWORK: CLOZE

Consult your notes to fill in the following blanks. Fill in each blank with a word which completes the meaning of the sentence. Use information you learned in the lecture, the context of the words, and your knowledge of grammar to help you.

Population of the United States

The most recent ______________ reveals that the present U.S. population is 241,000,000 people. This makes the United States the fourth most ______________ country in the world. The census divides the population into four groups by ______________ and origin: white, black, ______________ , and others. The largest group, white, ______________ 79% of the population. This census also shows that the East Coast is the most ______________ populated portion of the country, including five of the ______________ most populous states. The West, although ______________ densely populated, includes the most populous state, ______________. ______________ of the ten most populous states are located in the Midwest, and ______________ is the third most populous state. The average age of the U.S. population is 31.5, a figure which has been ______________ steadily in recent decades. This increase is due to two factors: a ______________ birth rate and a ______________ life span. It was also stated that there are about ______________ men for every 100 women in the population.

Follow-up: Check your answers with your teacher.

Foreign Students by World Region of Origin, 1954/55 – 1985/86

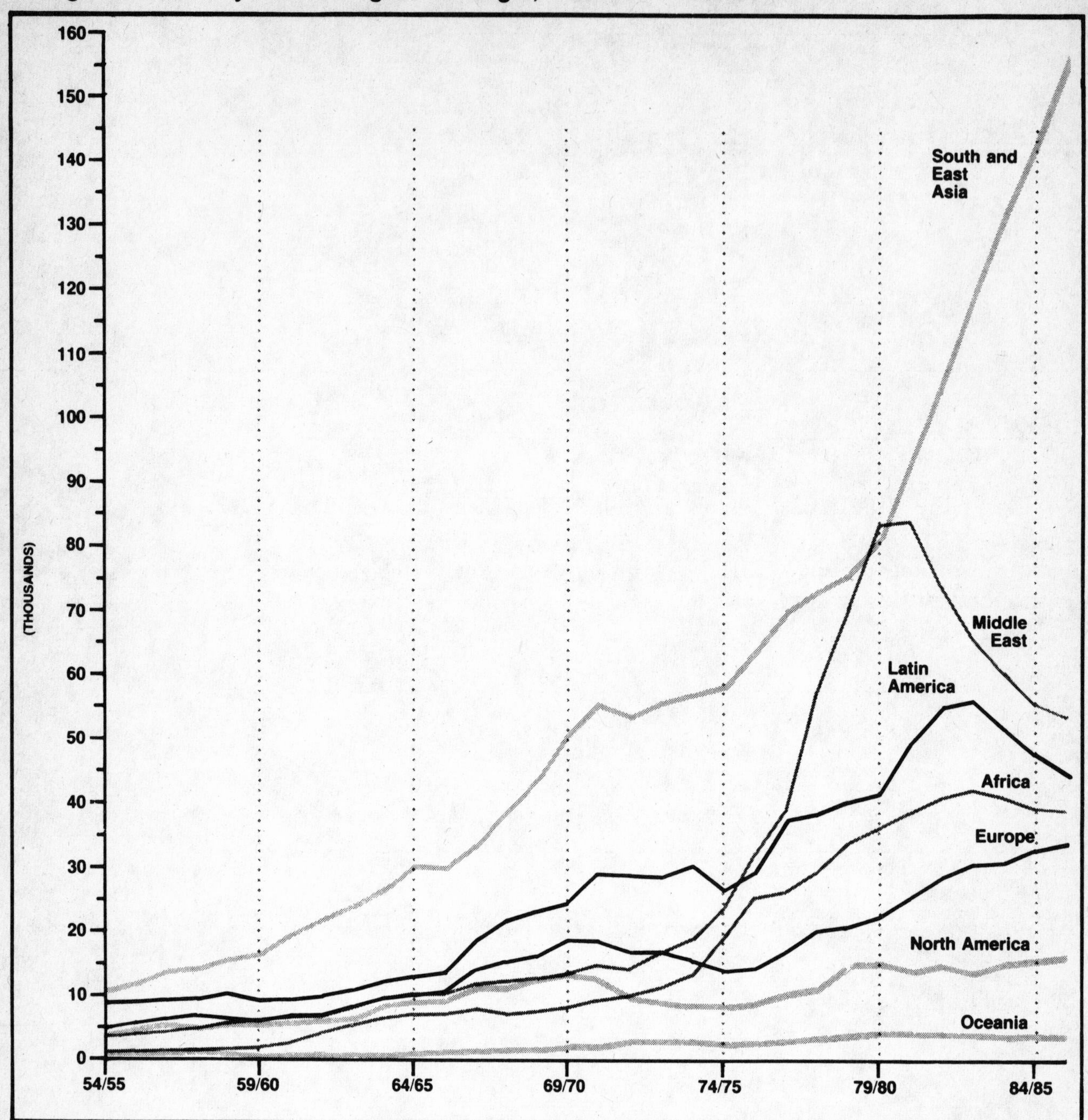

CHAPTER 2

Foreign Student Population

1. Prelistening Activities

A. PREDICTIONS

Using the title of the lesson and the illustration as a starting point, share with your classmates what you already know or think about this topic. Then write three questions you think will be answered in this lecture.

1. ______________________________

2. ______________________________

3. ______________________________

Follow-up: After you have written your questions, share your questions with your teacher and your classmates.

B. VOCABULARY AND KEY CONCEPTS

Write the word or words you hear in the blanks provided in each sentence.

1. In the academic year 1984/85 there was a small increase in the foreign student population in the United States.

2. Each year there are more foreign students in the United States. However, at the same time, the ___(rate)___ ___(of)___ ___increase___ has been getting smaller.

3. The foreign student population has been growing for a number of years, but the rate of growth has ___(dropped)___ ___(sharply)___ in recent years.

4. The ___(field)___ of engineering is the single most popular area of study for foreign students in the United States.

5. Most students receive a Bachelor of Arts or a Bachelor of Science degree after four years of ___undergraduate___ study.

6. Many foreign students are studying at the ___graduate___ level either for a Master's degree or a Ph.D.

7. Some students who are not interested in entering a profession attend a ___junior___ college for two years; others go to a technical school or another school offering ___non___-___degree___ programs.

8. Students in engineering ___account___ ___for___ over one fifth of all foreign students in the United States.

Follow-up: Check the spelling of the dictated words with your teacher. Discuss the meanings of these words and any other unfamiliar words in the sentences.

C. NOTETAKING SKILLS

Proper Notation with Numbers

During today's talk you will need to write down many numbers. Some of these will be expressed as whole numbers, some as percentages, some as fractions, and one will be a ratio. Let's do a little practice before the lecture. Here are some examples: If you hear "three fourths," you should write this *fraction* as $\frac{3}{4}$. If you hear "one out of six," you should write this *ratio* as 1:6. If you hear "thirteen point four percent," you should write this *percentage* as 13.4%. Let's practice.

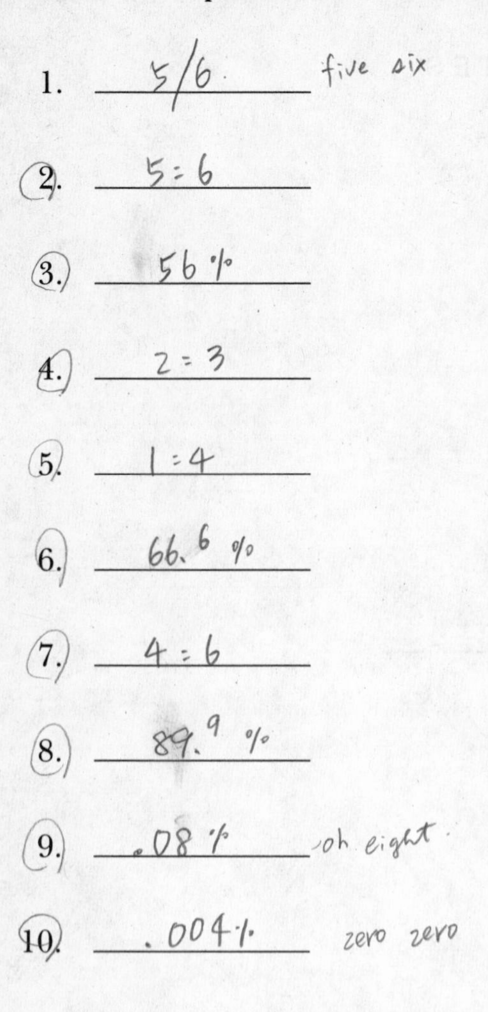

1. ____________
2. ____________
3. ____________
4. ____________
5. ____________
6. ____________
7. ____________
8. ____________
9. ____________
10. ____________

Follow-up: Check your answers with your teacher by reading them aloud.

2. Listening

A. FIRST LISTENING

Listen for general ideas. After a rather long introduction in which the lecturer discusses the overall decline in the rate of increase in foreign students in the United States and talks about how the foreign student population from some areas is declining while it is increasing from other areas, he lists three main subtopics, and then goes on to discuss each one individually. As you listen, write down the three major subtopics in the spaces under ST 1, ST 2, and ST 3 below.

LECTURE

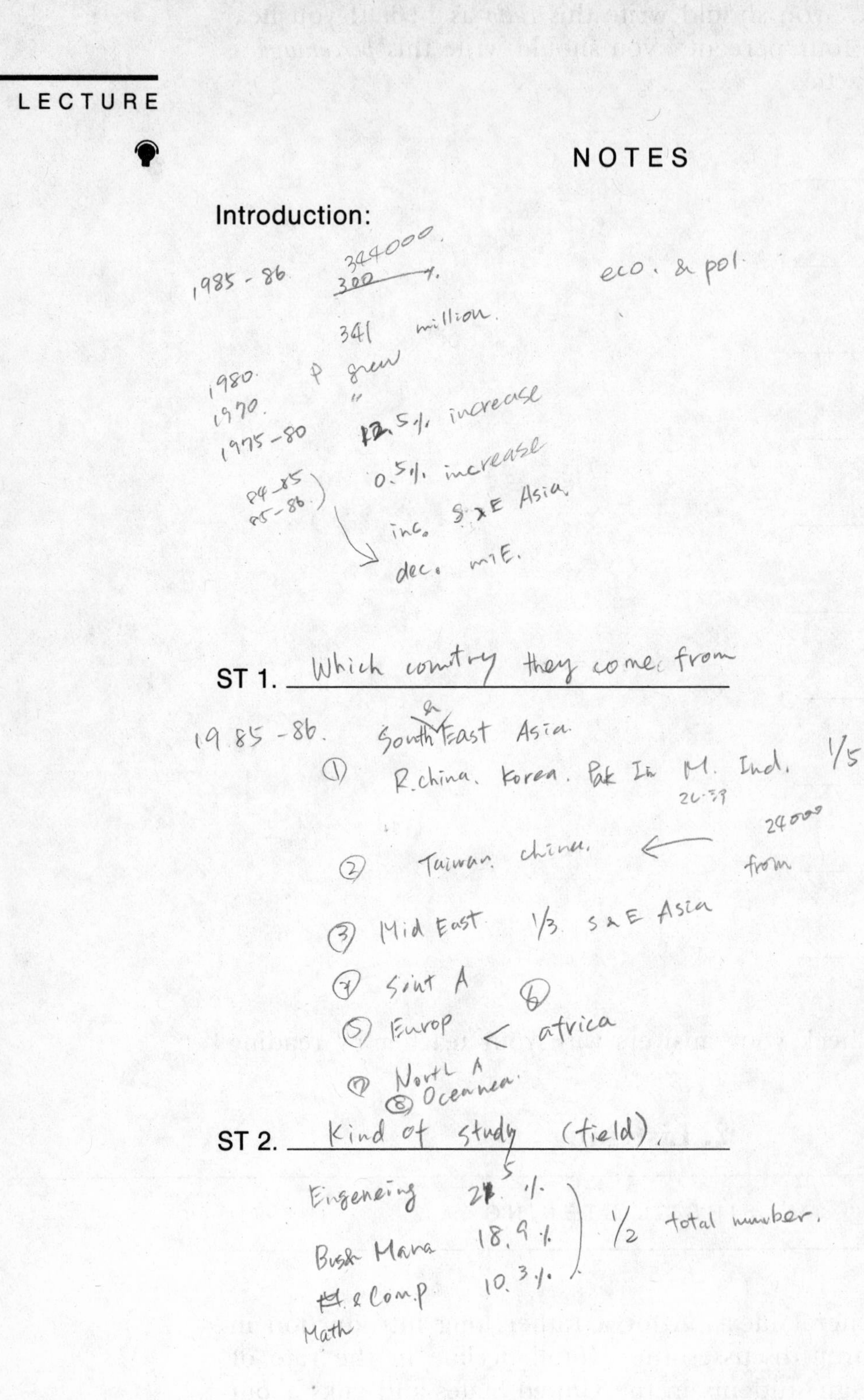

NOTES

Introduction:

ST 1.

ST 2.

ST 3. Academic level

Undergraduate 158 000
graduate 122 000
Jun & non-degree 2.7 % all population student of America) US institution
8.7 % graduate "

Follow-up: Now check your major subtopics with your teacher.

B. SECOND LISTENING

While listening again, write down as many relevant details as possible below the subtopics with which they belong.

LECTURE

Follow-up: Check your notes. Do you see places where you think you missed important information? If you had difficulty getting the important information, you may need more practice writing down the different forms of numbers. This is a good time to check to see if the lecturer answered your questions.

C. THIRD LISTENING

This time try to complete your notes while checking the ones you already have. Before the lecture begins, check your notes to see where you think you have missing information.

LECTURE

Follow-up: Keeping in mind that you will use your notes for a comprehensive quiz later on, compare your notes with your teacher's or your classmates'. Do you need to listen to the lecture again?

3. Postlistening Activities

A. ACCURACY CHECK

Listen to the following questions and circle the letter of the best answer. You may use your notes. You will hear each question one time only.

1. a. 241,000,000
   b. .5%
   c. 344,000
   d. 12.5%
2. a. 12.5%
   b. 21.7%
   c. .5%
   d. 18.9%
3. a. It dropped sharply.
   b. It grew rapidly.
   c. It was the same as in the 1970s.
   d. It grew a little more slowly than during the 1970s.
4. a. the Middle East
   b. Africa
   c. South and East Asia
   d. Europe
5. a. almost 24,000
   b. about 52,000
   c. 2 out of every 5
   d. 256,830
6. a. Europe
   b. the Middle East
   c. South and East Asia
   d. Oceania
7. a. business
   b. engineering
   c. mathematics and computer science
   d. management
8. a. graduate school
   b. undergraduate school
   c. junior colleges
   d. non-degree programs

9. a. 21.7%
   b. 2.7%
   c. 8.7%
   d. 122,000
10. a. origins of foreign students
    b. the names of the universities they study at
    c. the academic fields they pursue
    d. the academic levels they are found in

Follow-up: Check your answers with your teacher. If you had less than 70% of your answers correct, you should listen to the lecture again and check the accuracy and completeness of your notes.

B. ORAL PRACTICE

B.1. Review: Working in pairs, use your notes to practice giving sections of the lecture to each other. Student A will present the introduction and subtopic 1 and its details to Student B. Student B will present subtopics 2 and 3 and their details to Student A. Following his or her own notes, the student who is listening should check the accuracy and completeness of his or her partner's presentation.

Follow-up: Were your notes complete and accurate enough for you to do this oral practice activity with relative ease? Did you and your partner agree on essential information? If not, you may need to listen to the lecture again.

B.2. Transfer: Discuss with your teacher or a partner the following topics dealing with students from your country who go to other countries to study:

1. Which countries do students from your country go to to study?
2. Which fields do most of these students study in?
3. Why do these students go to these particular countries to study?

C. HOMEWORK: CLOZE

Consult your notes to fill in the following blanks. Fill in each blank with a word which completes the meaning of the sentence. Use information you learned in the lecture, the context of the words, and your knowledge of grammar to help you.

Origins of Foreign Student Population in the United States

While foreign student flows from most world regions __________ from 1984/85 to 1985/86, the flow from South and East Asia was substantially higher. With a rate of __________ of 9.2%, South and East Asian students __________ almost half (45.6%) of the total foreign student population in the United States last year, __________ from 42.0% in 1984/85. The next largest regional subgroup of foreign students, the Middle Easterners, was only a __________ of the South and East Asians. There were 52,720 foreign students from the Middle East, comprising 15.3% of all foreign students. Latin America was the region of __________ of 13.2%, or 45,480 students, while 10.0%, or 34,310, of the foreign students came from Europe and 9.9%, or 34,190 students, came from Africa. Europe was the only other world region that sent substantially __________ students, 2.9%, or 960, in 1985/86 than in the previous year. Flows from the other regions continued __________ decline: The flow from Africa __________ by 13.5%, that from the Middle East decreased by 6.8%, and that from Latin America fell __________ 6.3%.

Open Doors: 1985/86, New York: Institute of International Education, 1986, p. 1.

Follow-up: Check your answers with your teacher. Be sure to ask if you do not understand why one of your answers is wrong.

BONUS This lecture uses numbers in many forms. Complete the following table of percentages, fractions, and ratios. Check your answers with your teacher, *reading each one aloud.* The words in parentheses are provided as a guide to reading percentages, fractions, and ratios.

	Percentage	*Fraction*	*Ratio*
1.	50% (fifty percent)	½ (one half)	1 : 2 (one out of two)
2.	33%	______________	______________
3.	______________	¼ (one fourth)	______________
4.	______________	______________	2 : 5 (two out of every five)
5.	66.6%	______________	______________
6.	______________	9/10 (nine tenths)	______________

Of course, foreign students can be found virtually all over the States, but there are higher concentrations of them in certain areas. As you might expect, the three states with the highest number of foreign students are California, New York, and Texas. Large numbers of foreign students also study in Illinois and Michigan as well as in Massachusetts, Florida, and Pennsylvania.

Follow-up: Check your answers with your teacher.

GENERAL PUTNAM

CHAPTER 3

Immigration: Past and Present (Challenge Lesson)

1. Prelistening Activities

A. PREDICTIONS

Using the title of the lesson and the illustration as a starting point, share with your classmates what you already know or think about this topic. Then write three questions you think will be answered in this lecture.

1. ______________________

2. ______________________

3. ______________________

Follow-up: After you have written your questions, share your questions with your teacher and your classmates.

B. VOCABULARY AND KEY CONCEPTS

Write the word or words you hear in the blanks provided in each sentence.

1. Throughout history, people have moved, or immigrated, to new countries to live.

2. ______ ______ can take many forms: those which are characterized by a shortage of rain or food are called ______ and ______, respectively.

3. Sometimes people immigrate to a new country to escape political or religious ______.

4. Rather than immigrants, the early ______ from Great Britain considered themselves ______; they had left home to settle new land for the mother country.

5. The so-called Great Immigration, which can be divided into three ______, or time periods, began about 1830 and lasted till about 1930.

6. The Industrial Revolution, which began in the nineteenth century, caused ______ ______ as machines replaced workers.

7. The ______ of farmland in Europe caused many people to immigrate to the United States where farmland was more abundant.

8. Land in the United States was plentiful and available when the country was ______ westward. In fact, the U.S. government offered free public land to ______ in 1862.

9. The ______ of the Irish potato crop in the middle of the nineteenth century caused widespread starvation.

10. The Great Depression of the 1930s and World War II contributed to the noticeable ______ in immigration after 1930.

11. Although the U.S. government has __________ the number of immigrants ever since the Chinese Exclusion Act of 1882, __________ to the limits are sometimes made.

12. Exceptions to immigration laws have been made occasionally in cases where wars or other __________ displaced people from their own countries. Most recently, the U.S. government has felt a responsibility to accept __________ from Vietnam and Cuba, for example.

13. The U.S. immigration laws of today in general require that new immigrants have the __________ necessary to succeed in the U.S. because industry no longer requires large numbers of __________ workers.

Follow-up: Check the spelling of the dictated words with your teacher and discuss the meanings of these words and any other unfamiliar words in the sentences.

C. NOTETAKING PREPARATION

The lecturer uses the names of several countries as well as the names of the people who come from those countries. Check your knowledge of these names by completing the following chart in three minutes. A knowledge of the names of these countries and their peoples will help you recognize them when you hear them. Ask your instructor to pronounce the names of these countries and their people before you listen to the lecture. You will probably want to abbreviate some of these names as you take notes.

Country	*People*
__________	French
Germany	__________
__________	Scotch-Irish
__________	Britons; the British

Country	*People*
Denmark	Danes
Norway	Norwegians
Sweden	Swedes
Greece	Greek
Italy	Italians
Spain	Spaniards
Portugal	Portuguese
China	Chinese
Philipines	Filipinos
Mexico	Mexicans
Korea	Korean
the West Indies	West Indians
India	Indian
U.S.S.R. Russia	Russians
Poland Polish	Poles

Follow-up: After you check your answers with your teacher, answer these questions: Which of the above countries are Scandinavian countries? Which are Southern European countries? Which are Eastern European countries? Check your answers with your teacher.

2. Listening

A. FIRST LISTENING

Listen for general ideas. After a rather long introduction in which the lecturer discusses what immigration is, some general reasons that people immigrate, and the kinds of people who came to what is now the United States while it was still a colony of Great Britain, he goes on to discuss three main subtopics. He concludes his talk by discussing immigration today in the United States. As you listen, write down the three major subtopics under ST 1, ST 2, and ST 3.

LECTURE

NOTES

Introduction:

decline
emig V. < limit – defeent part
" – 1882 (中国)
economi 1929
cal.

ST 1. economical and political persequation

democration, renovent
Settlers, Colonist – Briton, Denmark. Finland, German, Scoltand / Irish
1776 40% Non British 76% others
Collonial 1830 – 1930 Great immigration
3 stages
1830 – 1860 10,000/year (G. B. I)
1860 – 1890 100,000 (D. N. S)
1890 – 1930 22 000 000 (E. B. R)
(SE. G. L. P)

ST 2. natural desaster

1. population – double in Europe decline
2. Industrial revolution (1832)
3. Improve ocean transport
4. plenty of labour and expanded employment in U.S.A.
5. economic laws

1716 – British report

ST 3.

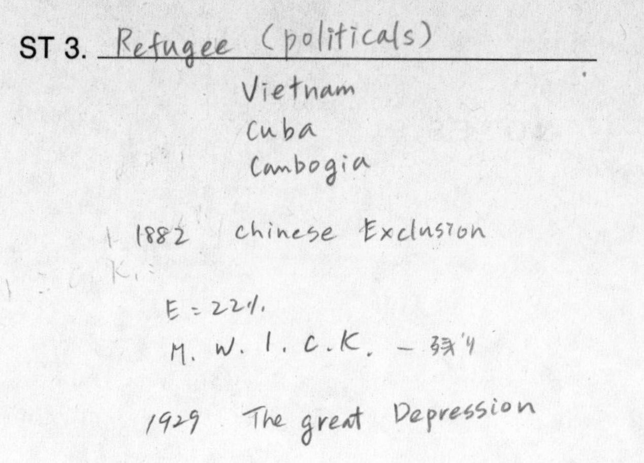

Conclusion:

Follow-up: Now check your major subtopics with your teacher.

B. SECOND LISTENING

While listening again, write down as many relevant details as possible below the main subtopic with which they belong.

LECTURE

Follow-up: Check your notes. Do you see places where you think you missed important information? If you had difficulty getting the important information, you may be writing down unimportant or irrelevant information. Try to get the important ideas first.

Much of what the lecturer says is repetitive. Listen for when he repeats or summarizes to check your notes. This is now a good time to see if the lecturer has answered the three prediction questions you wrote.

C. THIRD LISTENING

This time try to complete your notes while checking the ones you already have. Before you listen again, check your notes to see where you think you have missing information.

LECTURE

Follow-up: Keeping in mind that you will use your notes for a comprehensive quiz later on, compare your notes with your teacher's or your classmates'. Do you need to listen to the lecture again?

3. Postlistening Activities

A. ACCURACY CHECK

A.1. Listen to the following questions and circle the letter of the best answer. You will hear the question one time only. You may use your notes.

1. a. immigrants
   b. adventuresome
   c. restless
   d. settlers or colonists
2. a. French, Dutch, German
   b. French, Italian, Scotch-Irish
   c. German, Dutch, and Russian
   d. Scotch-Irish, Dutch, and Norwegian
3. a. non-Britons
   b. Britons
   c. 40%
   d. the majority

4. a. 10,000 a year
   b. 10,000,000
   c. 600,000
   d. 1,700,000
5. a. 1830–1860
   b. 1860–1890
   c. 1890–1930
   d. 1930–present
6. a. Eastern and Southern Europe
   b. Western Europe
   c. Northern Europe
   d. the British Isles
7. a. It decreased.
   b. It increased by 50%.
   c. It remained the same.
   d. It doubled.
8. a. 1776
   b. 1830
   c. 1862
   d. 1882
9. a. 1882
   b. 1914
   c. 1929
   d. 1930
10. Most immigrants are ________.
   a. Europeans
   b. non-Europeans
   c. rich and well-educated
   d. from countries with wars

Follow-up: Check your answers with your teacher.

A.2. Listen to the following statements. If the statement is true, put *T* in the space provided. If it is false, put *F*. You may use your notes if you like.

1. ______
2. ______
3. ______
4. ______
5. ______
6. ______
7. ______
8. ______
9. ______
10. ______

Follow-up: Check your answers with your teacher. If you had less than 70% of your answers to both quizzes correct, you should listen to the lecture again to check the accuracy and completeness of your notes.

B. ORAL PRACTICE

B.1. Review: Use your notes to practice giving one section of the lecture to one or more classmates. Take turns practicing different sections until everyone has had a chance to speak. For example, Student A will give the introduction, Student B will give subtopic 1, and so on. While another student is speaking, you should follow in your notes to see if he or she is accurate and complete.

Follow-up: Were your notes complete and accurate enough for you to do this oral practice activity with relative ease? If not, further listening to the lecture may be needed.

B.2. Transfer: Discuss with your teacher and classmates reasons why people either leave your country or come to your country. Do people leave your country for economic reasons? for educational reasons? Do they usually return home? Do people come to your country to work or to study? If so, who are these people? Do any of these people become citizens? How long do they stay in your country? What are some of the benefits of having immigrants in a country? What are some of the disadvantages?

C. HOMEWORK: READING COMPREHENSION

Read the following passage and answer the true-false questions which follow.

Immigration to Argentina

The original Europeans who settled Argentina in the 1500s were Spaniards, and today many Argentines trace their ancestry to Spain. Yet, while the 1869 census of Argentina showed that only twelve percent of the population were immigrants from other countries, half of the residents of Buenos Aires, the capital, were born in foreign countries. After 1880, the percentage of immigrants in the population grew rapidly. The largest number of immigrants entered Argentina during the decade 1901–1910. The decades 1921–30 and 1947–56 were also times of heavy immigration. Most of these immigrants came from Spain and Italy. A rather large number of Jews from Central Europe immigrated to Argentina during the Nazi era of the 1930s. After World War II, a significant number of refugees from Eastern Europe, especially Poland, also came to Argentina along with a sizable number of Middle-Easterners. To put the immigration picture in a larger world perspective, consider that of all the people who left Europe to immigrate to other countries between 1856 and 1937, eleven percent immigrated to Argentina. Today the vast majority of Argentines speak Spanish, but many also speak a second European language and there are four foreign-language newspapers published daily in Buenos Aires.

1. ______ According to the 1869 census, half of the population of Argentina lived in the capital city.

2. ______ Fewer immigrants entered Argentina between 1921–30 than between 1901–10.

3. ______ More people immigrated to Argentina from 1901 to 1910 than from 1947 to 1957.

4. ______ Most immigrants to Argentina were of European background.

Follow-up: Check your answers with your teacher.

COMPREHENSIVE QUIZ DIRECTIONS

Now that you have completed from one to three chapters in this unit, your teacher may wish you to take a comprehensive quiz on the chapter or chapters which you have completed. Your teacher will tell you whether or not you can use your notes to answer the questions on this quiz. If you can use your notes, you should review them before taking the quiz so that you can anticipate the questions and know where to find the answers. If you cannot use your notes, *study them carefully before you take the quiz,* concentrating on organizing the information into main ideas and details which support these main ideas.

Before you begin writing your answers, read all the questions carefully. Your answers should be accurate and complete but brief. Do not include any information which does not answer the questions. You may have abbreviations in your notes, but do not use abbreviations in your answers. For those questions which are preceded by an asterisk, you must write your answers in complete sentences.

UNIT II

The Face of the Land

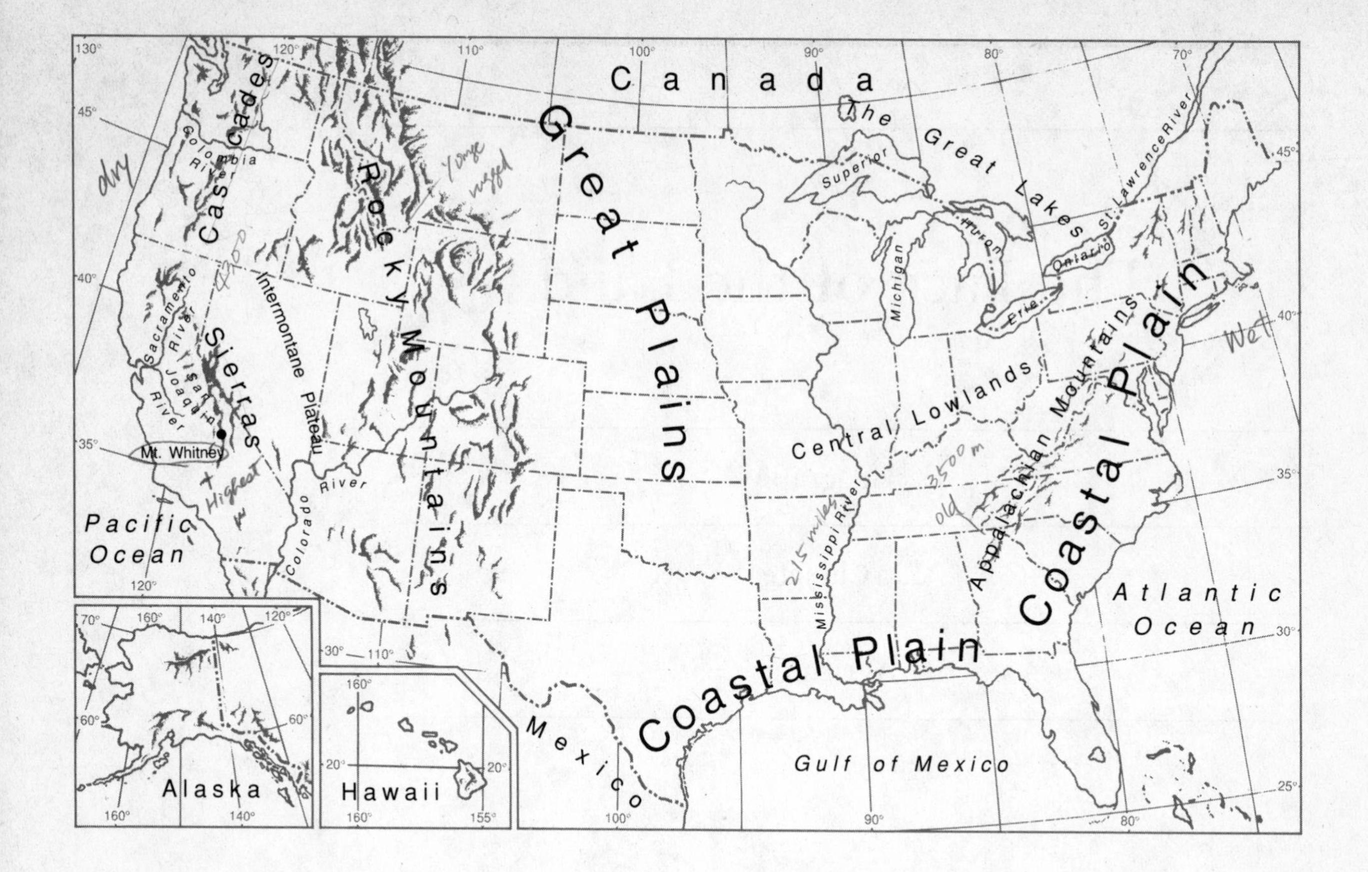
Canada
The Great Lakes
Superior
Michigan
Huron
Ontario
Erie
St. Lawrence River
Cascades
Columbia River
Rocky Mountains
Great Plains
Sacramento River
San Joaquin River
Sierras
Mt. Whitney
Intermontane Plateau
Colorado River
Pacific Ocean
Central Lowlands
Mississippi River
Appalachian Mountains
Coastal Plain
Atlantic Ocean
Gulf of Mexico
Mexico
Alaska
Hawaii

CHAPTER 4

Geography

1. Prelistening Activities

A. PREDICTIONS

Using the title of the lesson and the illustration as a starting point, share with your classmates what you already know or think about this topic. Then write three questions you think will be answered in this lecture.

1. ______________________________

2. ______________________________

3. ______________________________

Follow-up: After you have written your questions, share your questions with your teacher and your classmates.

B. VOCABULARY AND KEY CONCEPTS

Write the word or words you hear in the blanks provided in the following sentences.

1. The conterminous states are those that are located between the U.S. border with Mexico and Canada.

2. The three major mountain ________ generally ________ the country from north to south.

3. The Appalachian Mountains are ________ old, and, therefore, relatively low mountains.

4. The Rocky Mountains are younger, and, therefore, higher and more ________.

5. Mount Whitney is the highest ________ in the conterminous United States. Do you know what its ________ is?

6. A ________ is a flat, broad, raised area; on the other hand, a ________ is a level, treeless, often grassy region.

7. The interior ________ of the United States ________ a very large part of the country.

8. The Coastal Plain ________ from the southwestern United States to the Northeast.

9. If you look at the map, you will see that Florida is the only state that is a ________.

10. The Mississippi River is a ________ river which has its ________ near the Great Lakes.

11. Many ________ feed the Mississippi, which, in turn, ________ into the Gulf of Mexico.

12. The Great Lakes are ________ to the sea via the St. Lawrence River.

Follow-up: Check the spelling of the dictated words with your teacher and discuss the meanings of these words or any other unfamiliar words you don't understand.

C. NOTETAKING SKILLS

Using Visual Aids

Sometimes in a university lecture, you will have a graph, a table, or a map to look at. Usually when this kind of aid is available, looking at it even for a minute or two before the lecture will make it easier to understand the lecture. For this lecture, you have a map. Take a minute before the lecture to scan it in order to locate the major geographical features of the United States. Some of these words may be unfamiliar to you. You can use the map to check your spelling after you finish taking your notes.

2. Listening

A. FIRST LISTENING

Listen for general ideas. After a rather long introduction in which the lecturer discusses the relative size of the United States and the length of its borders, she goes on to mention the two major subtopics which she will discuss individually. As you listen, write down the two major subtopics under ST 1 and ST 2 below.

LECTURE

NOTES

Introduction:

climate. 3.6 million 9.6 Km

3000 miles.

4000 – Ca 2000 – M.

(1) Hy megion ranges and rivers

range

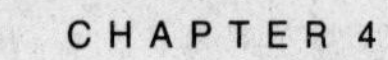

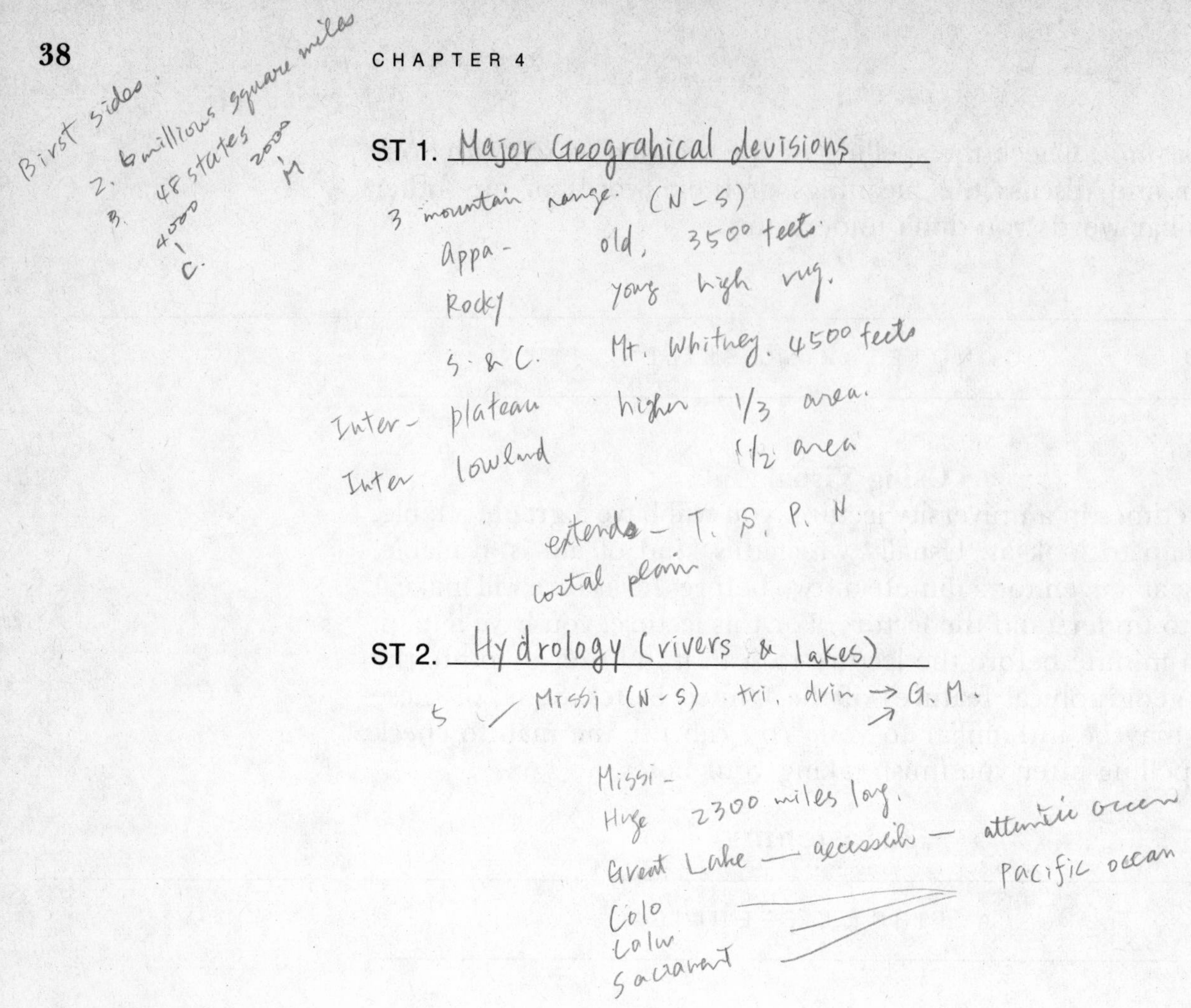

ST 1. ______________________________

ST 2. ______________________________

Follow-up: Check your major subtopics with your teacher.

B. SECOND LISTENING

While listening again, write as many of the relevant details as you can below the major subtopics with which they belong.

LECTURE

Follow-up: Check your notes. Do you see any places where you think you have missed important information? If you had difficulty getting the important information down, you may be trying to write sentences instead of taking notes. Write only enough information so that you can remember the ideas. Numbers are usually included in notes because they are almost always important information and difficult to remember without notes. This would be a good time to check to see if the lecturer answered your prediction questions.

C. THIRD LISTENING

This time try to complete your notes while also listening to the general ideas again.

LECTURE

Follow-up: Keeping in mind that you will use your notes for a comprehensive quiz later, compare your notes with your teacher's or with your classmates'. Do you need to listen to the lecture again?

3. Postlistening Activities

A. ACCURACY CHECK

Listen to the following statements. Put *T* in the space provided if the statement is true. Put *F* if it is false.

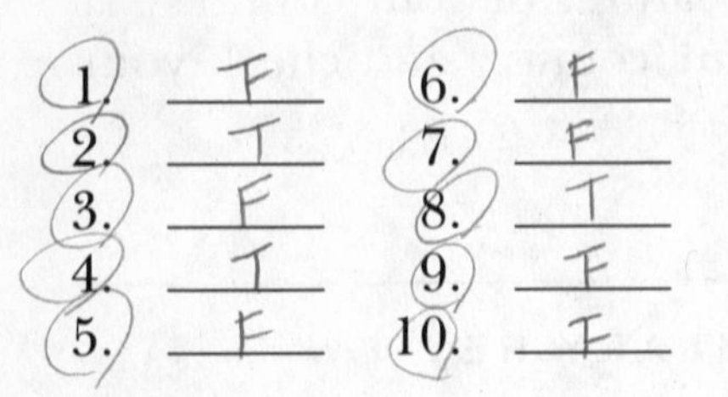

Follow-up: Check your answers with your teacher. If you had less than 70% correct, you should listen to the lecture again.

B. ORAL PRACTICE

B.1. Review: Working in pairs, use your notes to practice giving sections of the lecture to each other. Student A will present the introduction to Student B. Student B will present subtopic 1 and its details to Student A. Finally Student B will present subtopic 2 and its detail to Student A. Be sure that all of the following are included: borders, mountain ranges, lowlands, plains, plateaus, rivers, and lakes. Following his or her own notes, the student who is listening should check the accuracy and completeness of his or her partner's presentation.

Follow-up: Were your notes complete and accurate enough for you to do this oral practice activity with relative ease? Did you and your partner agree on essential information? If not, you may need to listen to the lecture again.

B.2. Transfer: Draw a simple map of your country. Then describe its major geographical features to a classmate or to your class. Begin your talk with the major geographical divisions and conclude it with the hydrology. Tell about as many of the following features of your country as you can:

Borders: with which countries, how long
Mountain ranges: where they are located, directions they traverse country, elevation, major peaks
Deserts, plains, plateaus, lowland: size, location
Lakes: location, size, accessibility to sea
Rivers: where the sources are, where they drain, how long they are, whether they are navigable, and in which direction they traverse country

Follow-up: Were you able to draw a simple map and put in at least some of the major geographical features of your country? If you had difficulty, locate a map of your country and check your work.

C. HOMEWORK: VOCABULARY REVIEW

Fill in the following blanks with vocabulary from the Vocabulary and Key Concepts exercise.

1. Alaska and Hawaii are not part of the conterminous United States.

2. The Rockies are ________ younger than the Appalachians.

3. It's a long way from the ____________ of the Mississippi to the Gulf of Mexico.

4. The U.S. ____________ with Canada is almost 4,000 miles long.

5. The Mississippi has many ____________, which help to explain its huge size.

6. Because the St. Lawrence River is ____________, ships are able to use it to reach the Great Lakes.

7. One difference between a plain and a plateau is that a ____________, generally speaking, has no trees.

8. The Mississippi River ____________ the country from north to south.

Follow-up: Check your answers with your teacher.

BONUS Complete the following passage on the geography of Zaire using the words from the following list:

access	area	consists	covered
drains	elevation	larger	longest
mountains	occupies	populated	

Zaire's vast ____________ of approximately 905,500 square miles makes it the third largest African country after the Sudan and Algeria. Zaire's land ____________ mainly of three major geographical types: (1) tropical rain forest, (2) savanna, and (3) highland. The tropical rain forest is found in the north and is one of the world's largest and densest. Because of the dense vegetation and high heat and humidity, the area is not very densely ____________. Much of southern Zaire is ____________ by savannas, which are grasslands and groups of trees. The highlands occupy the eastern and southwestern parts of Zaire. These highlands consist of plateaus and ____________, the highest of which is Margherita Peak with an ____________ of 16,762 feet. Zaire's major waterway is the Congo River (called the Zaire River in Zaire). Although it is the world's fifth ____________ river, it carries more water than any river except for the Amazon. The Congo

____________ into the Atlantic Ocean through Zaire's narrow ____________ to the sea in the southwest, which is only about twenty-five miles wide. The Congo river basin, with an altitude of about 1,000 feet, covers about one-third of the northern part of Zaire.

Follow-up: Check your answers with your teacher.

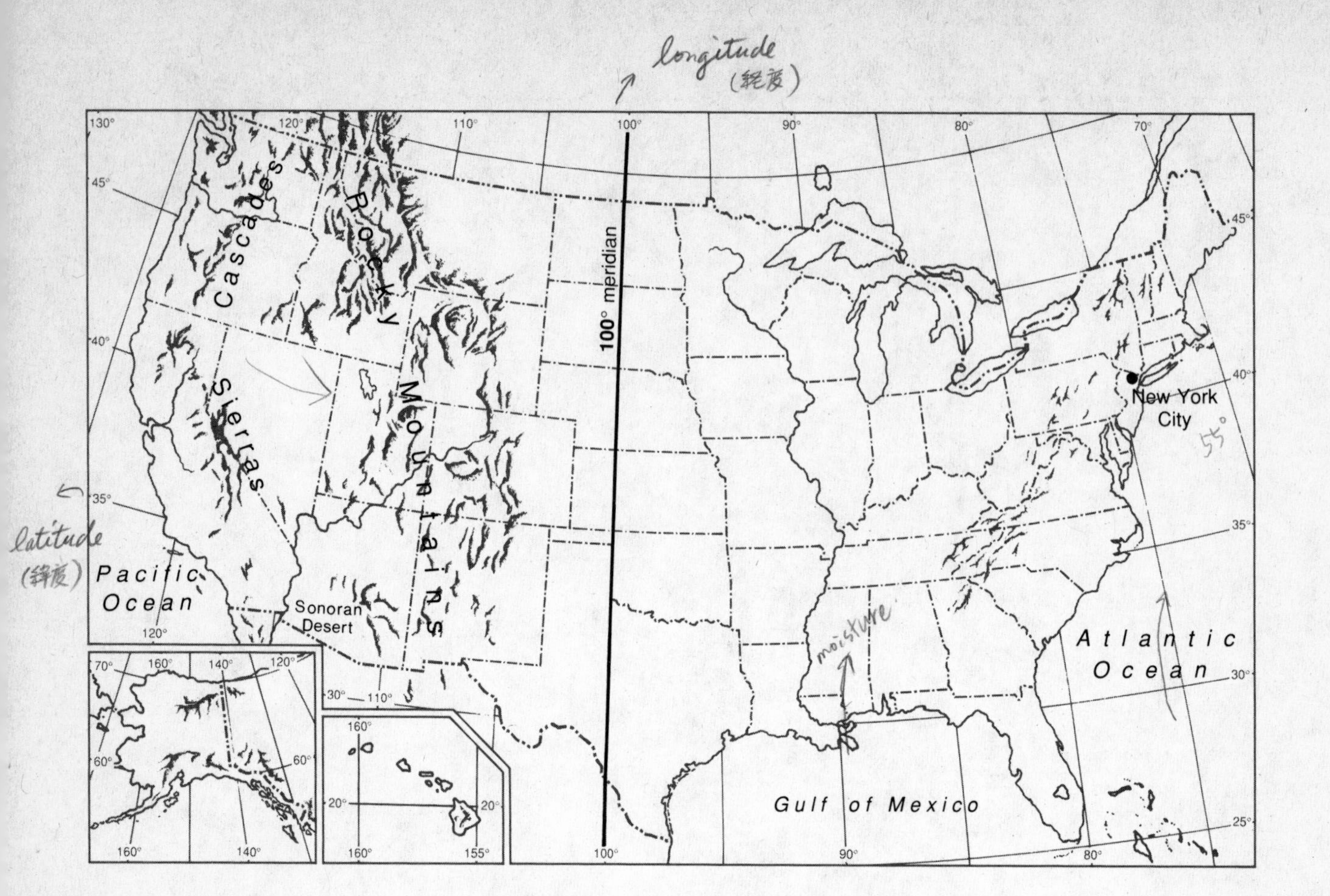
Cascades
Sierras
Rocky Mountains
100° meridian
Pacific Ocean
Sonoran Desert
New York City
Atlantic Ocean
Gulf of Mexico

CHAPTER 5

Climate

1. Prelistening Activities

A. PREDICTIONS

Using the title of the lesson and the illustration as a starting point, share with your classmates what you already know or think about this topic. Then write three questions you think will be answered in this lecture.

1. ______________________________

2. ______________________________

3. ______________________________

Follow-up: After you have written your questions, share your questions with your teacher and your classmates.

B. VOCABULARY AND KEY CONCEPTS

Write the word or words you hear in the blanks provided in the following sentences.

1. Any place on the face of the earth can be identified by its longitude and latitude.

2. The eastern United States is generally ____________ while the western United States is comparatively dry.

3. The annual ____________ rate is based on the amount of snow, rain, or hail that falls in one year.

4. Warm, ____________ air comes up from the Gulf of Mexico. In other words, this air is ____________ - ____________.

5. Winters in Florida and southern California are short and ____________.

6. The United States and Great Britain use the Fahrenheit scale to express ____________.

7. Warm air ____________ from the south and meets cold air ____________ flowing from the north.

8. High mountain ranges cause moist air masses to ____________ their moisture in the form of rain, hail, or snow.

9. The ocean has a ____________ effect on the climate of coastal areas.

10. The eastern part of the United States is, ____________ ____________ ____________, more humid than the western part.

11. On the whole, the United States has a ____________ climate.

Follow-up: Check the spelling of the dictated words with your teacher. Discuss the meanings of these words and any other unfamiliar words in the sentences.

C. NOTETAKING SKILLS

Using Visual Aids

For today's lecture, you also have a map to help you follow the lecture. Be sure you understand what longitude and latitude mean. Which do you think has the greatest effect on climate—longitude or latitude? Why?

Longitude and latitude, as well as temperature, are expressed in degrees. The symbol for degrees is a small circle written to the right of the number and above the line. Fahrenheit and Celsius are usually abbreviated as F and C. For example "ninety degrees Fahrenheit or twenty-four degrees Celsius" is written "90° F or 24° C."

2. Listening

A. FIRST LISTENING

Listen for general ideas. After an introduction in which the lecturer mentions the great varieties of climate types which are found in the United States, she goes on to say that she will discuss the climate of the United States under two major subtopics only. As you listen, write down the two major subtopics under ST 1 and ST 2 below.

LECTURE

NOTES

Introduction:

△ There are 15 kinds of climate in the world.
△ America has 11 divisions in continuous + 3 divisions in Hawai & Alaska.
△ Longitude and latitude effect on climate

ST 1. Eastern - half climate

humid (effected by G of M)
Short summer & long winter
moderate
no mountains
temparature change from N to S
20 inches (1512 milimeter)

ST 2. Western - half climate

dry
changeable
mountain area - snow
desert area - hot
125 - 2500

Follow-up: Were you able to get the two major subtopics? Check with your teacher.

B. SECOND LISTENING

This time as you listen to the lecture, take down in note form as many relevant details as possible below the major subtopic with which they belong.

LECTURE

Follow-up: Were you able to write down most of the relevant details? Do you see any places where you missed important information? This is a good place to check to see if the lecturer answered your prediction questions.

C. THIRD LISTENING

This time as you listen, try to fill in any information that you missed before. Before you listen to the lecture, check your notes to see where you think you may have missing information.

LECTURE

Follow-up: Keeping in mind that you will use your notes later for a comprehensive quiz, compare your notes with your teacher's or your classmates'. Do you need to listen to the lecture again?

3. Postlistening Activities

A. ACCURACY CHECK

For numbers 1–5 listen to the following questions and circle the letter of the best answer.

1. a. 14 11+3 conterminous
   b. 15
   c. 11
   d. 3
2. the ________
   a. Mississippi
   b. Rockies
   c. 100th meridian
   d. Coast Ranges
3. a. elevation
   b. latitude
   c. proximity to large bodies of water
   d. a, b, and c
4. the ________
   a. Sonoran Desert
   b. South
   c. New England
   d. West

5. It is ____________ than the eastern part.
   a. more changeable
   b. more humid
   c. hotter
   d. drier

For numbers 6–10 listen to the following statements. If the statement is true, write *T* in the space provided. If the statement is false, write *F*.

6. T
7. T (F)
8. T
9. F
10. T

Follow-up: Check your answers with your teacher. If you had less than 70% correct, you should listen to the lecture again.

B. ORAL PRACTICE

B.1. Review: Working in pairs, use your notes to practice giving sections of the lecture to each other. Student A will present the introduction and subtopic 1 and its details to Student B. Student B will present subtopic 2 and its details to Student A. Following his or her own notes, the student who is listening should check the accuracy and completeness of his or her partner's presentation.

Follow-up: Were your notes complete and accurate enough for you to do this oral practice activity with relative ease? Did you and your partner agree on essential information? If not, you may need to listen to the lecture again.

B.2. Transfer: Using the map you drew of your country for the previous lesson on geography, tell your classmate about the climate of your country. If you feel that you don't know enough about the climate, consult an encyclopedia. Encourage your classmate to ask you questions after you have finished telling him or her about the climate in your country. If you are from the same country, you could prepare a short talk about the climate of your country that you would give to a person from another country who asked you about the climate of your country.

Follow-up: Were you able to tell your classmate about the climate in your country? If you are from different countries, did you learn something new about the climate of your classmate's country? Were you able to answer your classmate's questions? Were you able to ask him or her the questions that you wanted to? If so, you were both successful.

C. HOMEWORK: VOCABULARY REVIEW

Fill in the blanks with a word from the following list. Do not use any word more than one time.

annual	cold	elevation
highest	hot	inches
latitude	longitude	mild
moderates	plateaus	precipitation
temperature	warm	

Variety of Climates in the United States

Because the United States covers a vast territory extending from Alaska, part of which is inside the Arctic Circle, to Hawaii, which is close to the Tropic of Cancer, that is, from approximately the 70° to the 20° latitude, the United States has a great variety of climates.

Average ______ temperatures range from 78.2° F (25.7° C) in Death Valley, California, to 9° F (−13° C) in Barrow, Alaska. The ______ temperature ever recorded was 134° F (57° C) at Death Valley, in southwestern California, on July 10, 1913. The lowest temperature ever recorded was −79.8° F (−62.1° C) in Prospect Creek, Alaska, on January 23, 1971.

The average annual ______ rate varies from less than 2 inches (5 cm) at Death Valley to about 460 ______ (1,170 cm) at Mount Waialeale in Hawaii. Most parts of the country, however, experience seasonal changes in ______ and moderate precipitation.

Climate is greatly affected by ______. New England, for example, has ______ summers and long ______ winters while the South has long ______ summers and ______ winters. ______ also affect climate. In the West, mountainous areas are cooler and wetter than nearby plains and plateaus. Proximity (closeness) to the ocean or other large bodies of water moderates climate. This is why the climate along much of the Pacific coast is relatively mild all year.

Follow-up: Check your answers with a classmate. If one of you has written a different word in a blank, discuss your answers to try to decide which is correct. One or both of you should change your answer. After you have finished discussing your answers, check your answers with your teacher.

BONUS Label the following map of New England. The names of the six states and their abbreviations are listed for you. Write the name of the state or its abbreviation onto the correct state on the map. Listen carefully to the speaker.

Maine	Me.
New Hampshire	N.H.
Vermont	Vt.
Massachusetts	Mass.
Connecticut	Conn.
Rhode Island	R.I.

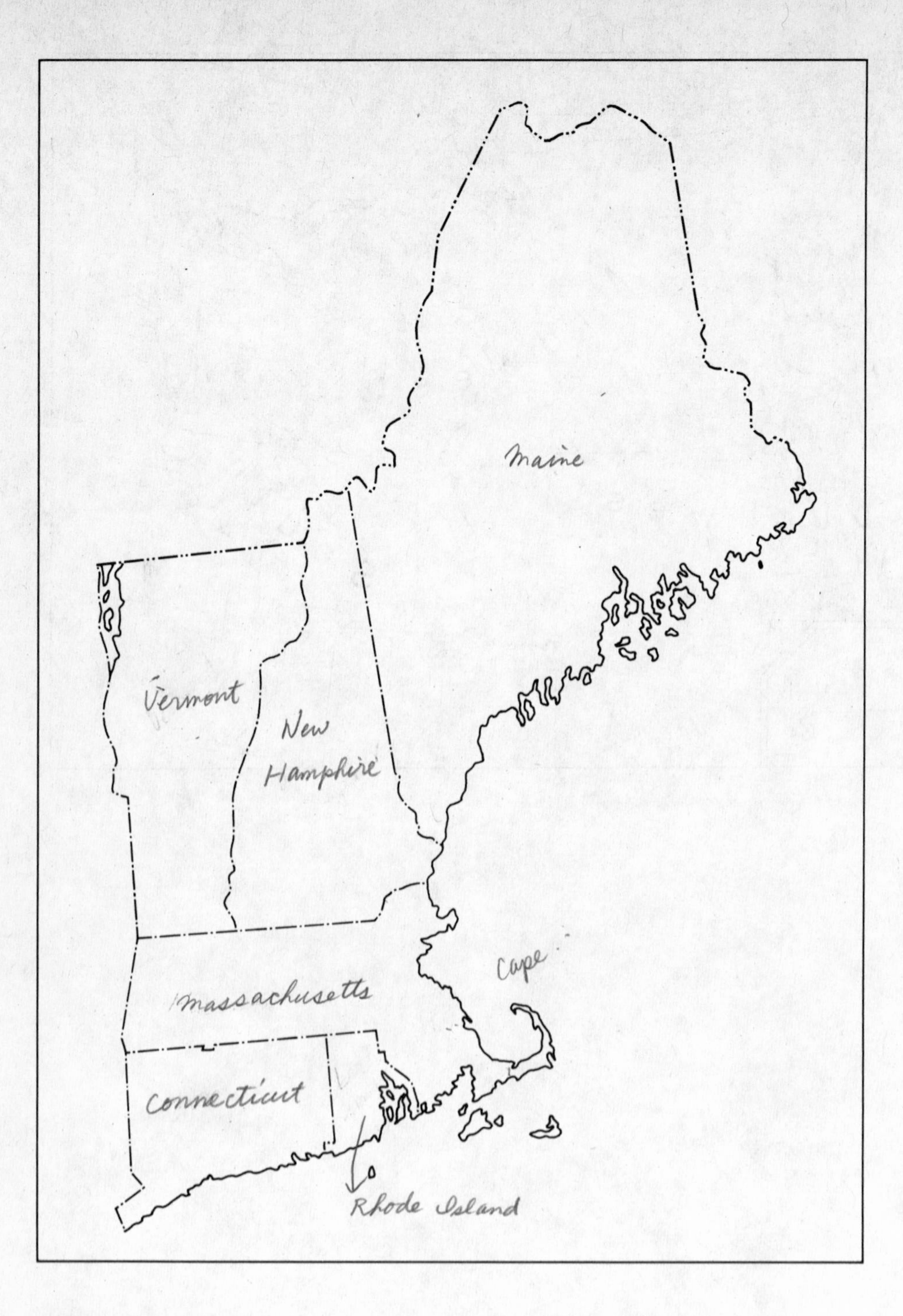

Follow-up: Check your answers with your teacher.

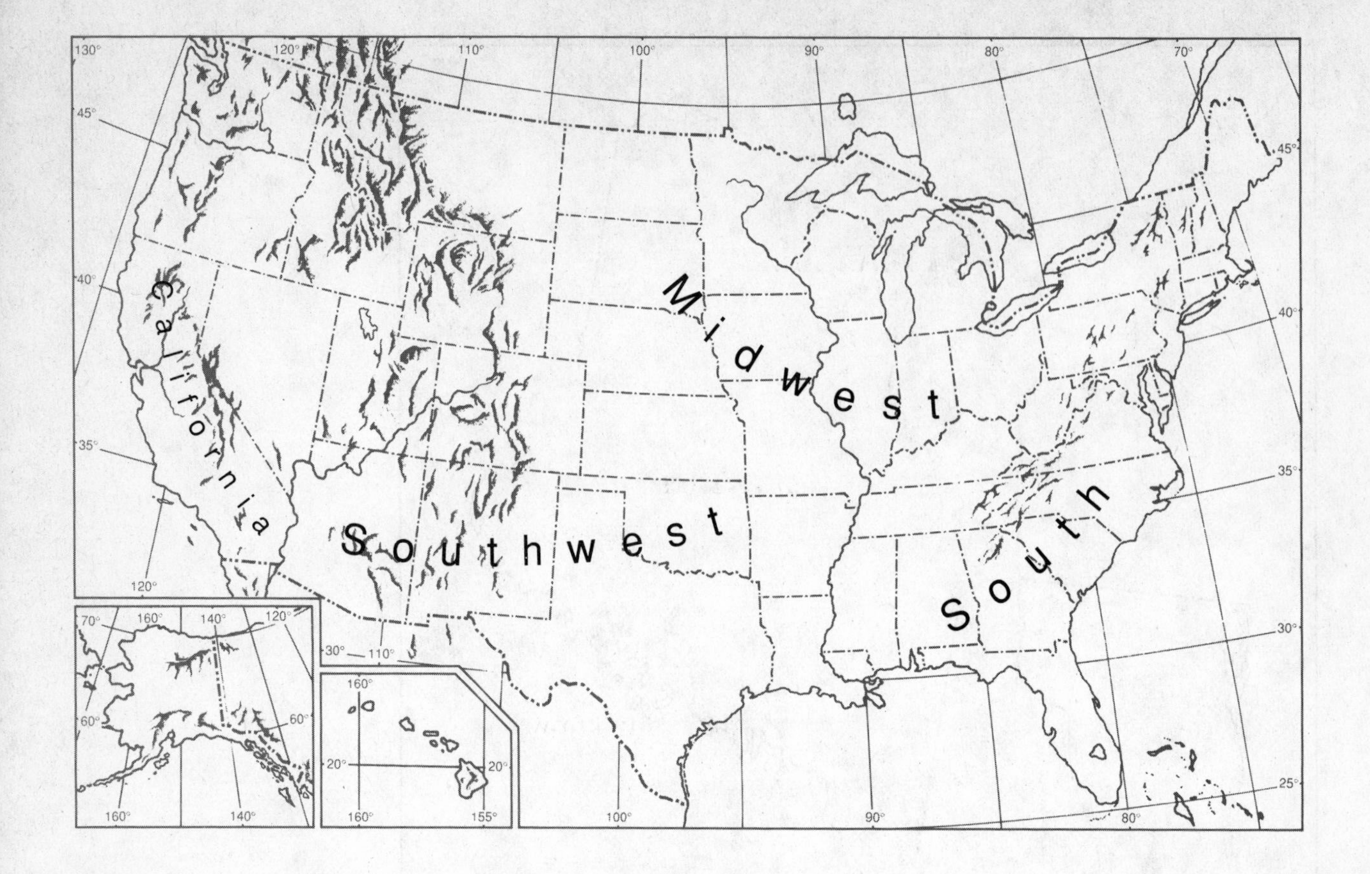
California
Southwest
Midwest
South

CHAPTER 6

Agriculture

1. Prelistening Activities

A. PREDICTIONS

Using the title of the lesson and the illustration as a starting point, share with your classmates what you already know or think about this topic. Then write three questions you think will be answered in this lecture.

livestock (animal)

1. ______________________________

2. ______________________________

3. ______________________________

Follow-up: After you have written your questions, share your questions with your teacher and your classmates.

B. VOCABULARY AND KEY CONCEPTS

Write the word or words you hear in the blanks provided in the following sentences.

1. A relatively small number of farmers produce an enormous quantity of ___crops___ and ___livestock___.

2. The average U.S. farm is 440 ___acres___, or 178 ___hectares___, in area.

3. The United States' high ___(productivity)___ in agriculture makes it one of the world's ___(leadings)___ ___exporters___ of food.

4. One reason for the productivity is an abundance of ___(fertile)___, flat land that doesn't require ___(irrigation)___.

5. Many agricultural products ___are___ ___raised___ in every part of the country.

6. ___(Dairy)___ products are produced mostly in the northern part of the country. (milk, cheese, yorgult) (Wisconshin)

7. Because agriculture is ___(mechanized)___, almost all planting and ___(harvesting)___ are done by machine.

8. Other evidence of technology in agriculture is the use of both chemical ___(fertilizers)___ and ___(pesticides)___ to increase productivity. (locust)

9. New ___(hybrid)___ grains and livestock are often more productive than ___traditional___ grains and livestock. (beefalo)

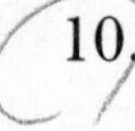

10. When farmers produce a ___surplus___ of agricultural products, there are enough products to be exported. (bumper crop)

Follow-up: Check the spelling of the dictated words with your teacher. Discuss the meanings of these words and any other unfamiliar words in the sentences.

C. NOTETAKING SKILLS

Recognizing Relevant Information

When a lecturer announces that he or she is going to enumerate (till reasons) reasons, examples, members of a category, and so forth, you can be fairly sure that this information is "noteworthy." In this lecture the speaker mentions *three* reasons for the high agricultural productivity in the United States, lists *eleven* major crops and where they are grown, and discusses *three* ways in which agricultural technolgoy is important. As you listen to the lecture, use these numbers to help you organize your notes and to check to see if you have all the important details.

2. Listening

A. FIRST LISTENING

Listen for general ideas. After a long introduction in which the lecturer mentions some general characteristics of U.S. farms and farmers, she says that she will look at agriculture in two ways. Write down these two major subtopics under ST 1 and ST 2 below.

LECTURE

NOTES

Introduction:

reasons
1 high temp & clim.
2 plate fertile irrigation
3 agricultural technology

3% few (80 people)
440 acres.
178 hectares.

crops
1. cattle & beef.
2 dairy product – N.
3 corns (grains) – M.
4 soybeen
5 wheat
6 hurt & pork
7 potry & egg
8 vegetable
9 fruit > Cal.
10 carton – S.W/Cal.
11 tobaco.

ways
1. mechanized
2. chemical fertilize & pesticide
3. hybrid gains

1 restrict to produce food
2 control price of food.

ST 1. ______________________________

ST 2. ______________________________

Conclusion:

Follow-up: Were you able to get the two major subtopics? Check with your teacher.

B. SECOND LISTENING

This time as you listen to the lecture, take down in note form as many relevant details as possible below the major subtopics with which they belong.

LECTURE

Follow-up: Were you able to get down most of the relevant details? Were you able to take notes on the three reasons for high agricultural productivity in the United States, the eleven major crops and where they are grown, and the three ways technology has affected U.S. agriculture? This would also be a good time to check to see if the lecturer answered your prediction questions.

C. THIRD LISTENING

Listen one more time to fill in any missing information. Look at your notes before the lecture begins to see where you have missing information.

LECTURE

Follow-up: Keeping in mind that you will use your notes for a comprehensive quiz later, compare your notes with your teacher's or your classmates'. Do you need to listen to the lecture again?

3. Postlistening Activities

A. ACCURACY CHECK

Listen to the following questions and write short answers.

1. 3%

2. 80 people

3. 178 hectares

4. grains temparate climate

6 ~~5.~~ crops & livestock

5 ~~6.~~ The United States has a great deal of flat, fertile land.

7. South W. / Cal.

8. harvesting & planting

9. fertilzer & pesticize

10. restrict land and ~~control~~ buy surplus price

Follow-up: Check your answers with your teacher. If you had less than 70% correct, you should listen to the lecture again and check the accuracy and completeness of your notes.

B. ORAL PRACTICE

B.1. Review: Working in pairs, use your notes to practice giving sections of the lecture to each other. Student A will present the introduction and subtopic 1 and its details to Student B. Student B will present subtopic 2 and its details to Student A. Following his or her own notes, the student who is listening should check the accuracy and completeness of his or her partner's presentation.

Follow-up: Were your notes complete and accurate enough for you to do this oral practice activity with relative ease? Did you and your partner agree on essential information? If not, you may need to listen to the lecture again.

B.2. Transfer: Take turns discussing with a classmate the agriculture in your country. If you are from different countries, it would be a good idea to compare your two countries. Include information on approximately what percentage of people in your countries are farmers, whether they mainly have large or small farms and grow food only for a few or for many people. Discuss the major crops grown in your countries. Which are for local use and which for export? What kinds of agricultural technology are used in your countries?

Follow-up: Were you able to discuss agriculture in your country fairly easily? Are there vocabulary words for certain crops or products that you don't know in English? This would be a good time to look them up in a bilingual dictionary.

C. HOMEWORK: VOCABULARY REVIEW

Complete the following passage using the following words:

acres	agricultural	beef
crops	dairy	farm
fertilizers	growing season	pasture
productive	raised	technological

Agriculture in Japan

Unlike the large U.S. farms, the average Japanese ____________ is only three ____________ (1.2 hectares) in area. The growing season varies from 250 or more days per year in the Southwest to 120 days in the North. Where the ____________ is longer, three successive ____________ can be raised in one year, but only one crop is possible where the season is shorter. Despite the small average size, Japanese farms are among the most ____________ per acre in the world. In fact about 70% of the food needed to feed the Japanese people is raised on about 15% of the land. Intensive ____________ techniques including irrigation, use of ____________, and terracing uneven land help to explain this high productivity. The major summer crop is rice, and other important crops have included wheat, barley, potatoes, and a large variety of vegetables. The major commercial crops are mulberry leaves, used as food for silkworms, and tea. Hydroponic gardening, a ____________ method using computers, is increasingly used to grow fruits and vegetables. Very little livestock is ______ raised ______, and, consequently, very little land is used as ______ pasture ______. However, in recent years the Japanese have developed an increasing taste for meat, particularly beef, for ______ dairy ______ products such as milk, and for eggs, so more farmers are raising ______ beef ______ and dairy cattle, chickens, and hogs. → piglet

Follow-up: Check your answers with your teacher.

BONUS Discuss the following issue with your classmates or your teacher: Although agricultural technology can increase agricultural production dramatically, it brings many problems with it. List as many of these problems as you can think of.

COMPREHENSIVE QUIZ DIRECTIONS

Now that you have completed from one to three chapters in this unit, your teacher may wish you to take a comprehensive quiz on the chapter or chapters which you have completed. Your teacher will tell you whether or not you can use your notes to answer the questions on this quiz. If you can use your notes, you should review them before taking the quiz so that you can anticipate the questions and know where to find the answers. If you cannot use your notes, *study them carefully before you take the quiz,* concentrating on organizing the information into main ideas and details which support these main ideas.

Before you begin writing your answers, read all the questions carefully. Your answers should be accurate and complete but brief. Do not include any information which does not answer the questions. You may have abbreviations in your notes, but do not use abbreviations in your answers. For those questions which are preceded by an asterisk, you must write your answers in complete sentences.

UNIT III

How the People Live (American Society)

CHAPTER 7

The Nuclear Family

1. Prelistening Activities

A. PREDICTIONS

Using the title of the lesson and the illustration as a starting point, share with your classmates what you already know or think about this topic. Then write three questions you think will be answered in this lecture.

1. ______________________________

2. ______________________________

3. ______________________________

Follow-up: After you have written your questions, share your questions with your teacher and your classmates.

B. VOCABULARY AND KEY CONCEPTS

Write the word or words you hear in the blanks provided in each sentence.

1. Although the ____________ family is well-known in many parts of the world, in the United States it is not a common family ____________ .

2. A ____________ family is one which consists of father and mother living together with their children in a separate ____________ .

3. The number of families ____________ by women with no husband present more than ____________ between 1960 and 1985.

4. Many of these families face great economic hardship with their ____________ ____________ less than 50% of ____________ households.

5. This means that many children will live with one natural parent and one ____________ in a ____________ family.

6. Now let's discuss some reasons that the nuclear family is so ____________ in the United States.

7. Usually they have left the older ____________ behind, which may in itself weaken the family structure to some ____________ .

8. As second and third generations become ____________ , they adopt the ____________ of the general society.

9. The westward movement ____________ the nuclear family because ____________ often had to leave behind most of their families.

10. Many older people are fairly ____________ ____________ and want to be able to ____________ their own interests.

11. That young people often live separately from their parents doesn't mean there is no ____________ between them.

Children usually ____________ closer relations with their parents when they get married or have a child.

12. The United States is a society which values ____________, independence, and ____________.

Follow-up: Check the spelling of the dictated words with your teacher. Discuss the meanings of these words and any other unfamiliar words in the sentences.

C. NOTETAKING SKILLS

Key Words

A good notetaker knows that it is neither efficient nor necessary to take down the lecture word for word. A good notetaker listens for relevant information and then uses key words to take down only the essential information. In other words, a good notetaker will *reduce* a whole sentence or even a whole paragraph into a few key words if possible. Practice reducing information to key words using the sentences from Vocabulary and Key Concepts. Do sentences 3, 8, 9, 10, and 11. Sentence 2 is done for you as an example.

2. Extended family well-known in world, *not* in U.S.

Note: Articles, auxiliaries, and the verb *to be* are usually not useful as key words.

3. ____

8. ____

9. ____

10. ____

11. ____

Follow-up: Two students should write their key words on the board for other students to comment on and to compare theirs with.

2. Listening

A. FIRST LISTENING

Listen for general ideas. The lecturer begins with a rather lengthy introduction which defines the nuclear family and gives some statistical information about the family in general. He concludes the introduction by mentioning the major subtopics which he goes on to develop in the lecture. Concentrate on main ideas for the first listening. Be sure to write the major subtopics in the appropriate place.

LECTURE

NOTES

Introduction:

ST 1. ______________________________

ST 2. ______________________________

ST 3. ______________________________

Conclusion:

Follow-up: Check your major subtopics with your teacher.

B. SECOND LISTENING

Using your key word strategy as much as possible, listen for relevant details to support the main subtopics. Leave some space between your notes so that you can fill in additional information in the third listening if necessary.

LECTURE

↺

Follow-up: Take a minute to look at your notes. Do you see places where you missed information? Did you write full sentences or did you use *key words* as instructed? This would be a good time to see if the lecturer answered your prediction questions.

C. THIRD LISTENING

Use the third listening to check the notes you already have and to fill in any relevant details that you didn't have time to get down before.

LECTURE

↺

Follow-up: Keeping in mind that you will use your notes for a comprehensive quiz later on, check your notes with your teacher's or with a classmate's. Do your notes have basically the same information? Do you believe your notes are complete enough? Go on to the Accuracy Check before deciding if you need to listen to the lecture again.

3. Postlistening Activities

A. ACCURACY CHECK

For numbers 1–5 listen to the following questions and write short answers.

1. ______________________________

2. ______________________________

3. ______________________________

4. ______________________________

5. ______________________________

For numbers 6 and 7 listen to the questions and circle the letter of the best answer.

6. a. nuclear
   b. extended
   c. blended
   d. single-parent
7. a. desire of older people to live separately
   b. "Americanization" of immigrants
   c. economic hardship
   d. westward movement

For numbers 8–10 listen to each statement and write *T* if it is true and *F* if it is false.

8. ______
9. ______
10. ______

Follow-up: Check your answers with your teacher. If you got less than 70% correct, you may need to listen to the lecture again. (If possible, try to make arrangements to listen again outside class.)

B. ORAL PRACTICE

B.1. Review: Take turns with a partner giving different sections of the lecture. For example, Partner A will give the introduction and the first subtopic about the nuclear family, and Partner B will talk about subtopics 2 and 3. Following his or her own notes, the student who is listening should check the accuracy and completeness of his or her partner's presentation.

Follow-up: Were your notes complete and accurate enough for you to do this oral practice activity with relative ease? Did you and your partner agree on essential information? If not, you may need to listen to the lecture again.

B.2. Transfer: Discuss the following questions as a class with your teacher:

1. Is the basic family pattern in your country nuclear or extended?
2. Is the family pattern in your country changing? Why?
3. What are the advantages of the extended family?
4. What are the advantages of the nuclear family?

C. HOMEWORK: READING COMPREHENSION

Read the following passage and answer the comprehension questions.

China: The Changing Family

Looking at the People's Republic of China before 1949, when the Communist Party under Chairman Mao took control of the country, and today, we see vast changes in the family, especially in the cities. Traditionally the desirable family was a big extended one, the ideal family having five generations and as many as one hundred people under one roof. Although rich landowners, merchants, and government officials could aspire to and attain such a large family, the common people lived in much smaller units in either a nuclear or limited extended pattern. Only men were expected to work outside the home, and the eldest male had complete authority over the household. Marriages were most often arranged by the parents.

Today the family unit is a smaller one although there may often still be a grandparent present. The government's attention to family planning, including the campaign launched in 1979 for the one-child family, has naturally reduced the size of the family. The Communist government encourages women to contribute politically, socially, and professionally, so women are no longer expected to stay at home. Indeed, almost all adults in China have a job. Relations between parents and children are more democratic than in the past, and children, especially in the cities, are more likely to marry the person of their choice, but probably after consulting their parents. Change is normal in any society, but these changes in the Chinese family are noteworthy for how quickly they have occurred since the revolution.

Comprehension Questions

1. Why are the changes in the Chinese family amazing?

   ____

2. What two time periods are compared?

   ____

3. How has the size of the family changed?

   ____

4. In what way has the role of women changed?

   ____

5. How have parent-child relations changed?

   ____

Follow-up: Check your answers with your teacher.

MILK

CHAPTER 8

Religion

1. Prelistening Activities

A. PREDICTIONS

Using the title of the lesson and the illustration as a starting point, share with your classmates what you already know or think about this topic. Then write three questions you think will be answered in this lecture.

1. ______________________________

2. ______________________________

3. ______________________________

Follow-up: After you have written your questions, share your questions with your teacher and your classmates.

B. VOCABULARY AND KEY CONCEPTS

Write the word or words you hear in the blanks provided in each sentence.

1. The 75,000,000 ____________ in the United States are found in more than 1,200 ____________.

2. Although only about 60% of the population are ____________ members of a church or synagogue, many of the other 40% identify with one of the major religious groups and occasionally attend religious ____________.

3. ____________ and Buddhism are more ____________ represented in the United States than are the three major religions that I've already mentioned.

4. ____________ by the Constitution, freedom of religion means basically that people can believe in and practice any religion they want to.

5. The right to religious freedom is not an ____________ one, and maybe it can't be in a very ____________ society like the United States.

6. For example, the Supreme Court, in ____________ a law against polygamy, ____________ the Mormons' religious freedom.

7. If there is separation of church and state in the United States, why do witnesses ____________ an ____________ on the Bible in court?

8. The Supreme Court recently ____________ prayer and other religious exercises in public schools.

9. Separation of church and state basically means the government must not ____________ any religious activities and religious groups must not ____________ in government.

10. There are some ____________, but, on the whole, separation of church and state works quite well in the United States.

11. In addition to social activities, many churches offer services such as nursery schools, after-school programs for older children, and opportunities for ____________ work for members in hospitals and nursing homes.

12. Even though people may not be regular church attenders, they usually want their children to be married by a priest, minister, or rabbi and will want religious services at the ____________ of a loved one.

Follow-up: Check the spelling of the dictated words with your teacher. Discuss the meanings of these words and any other unfamiliar words in the sentences.

C. NOTETAKING SKILLS

Key Words

In the first chapter of this unit you practiced reducing sentences to key words. For more practice read the conclusion to this lecture and reduce the information to notes using meaningful key words. Do not use more than 25 words!

"In conclusion, I would like to leave you with a few of my observations. Even though people may not be regular church attenders, they usually want their children to be married by a priest, minister, or rabbi and will want religious services at the funeral of a loved one. Judeo-Christian values are deeply imbedded in the culture, and most people, whether churchgoers or not, are deeply influenced by them."

Follow-up: Two students should go to the board and quickly write their notes for other students to comment on and to compare their notes with.

2. Listening

A. FIRST LISTENING

In the introduction the lecturer discusses the reasons for the great number of churches in the United States and follows with figures for church membership. At the end of the introduction he mentions the three subtopics he will go on to develop. Concentrate on the main ideas during the first listening. Be sure to write the three major subtopics in the appropriate places as you listen.

LECTURE

NOTES

Introduction:

ST 1. ______________________

ST 2. ______________________________

ST 3. ______________________________

Conclusion:

Follow-up: Check your major subtopics with your teacher before you listen to the lecture for the second time.

B. SECOND LISTENING

Continue using your key word strategy as you listen for relevant details to support the main subtopics. Once again leave space for additional information in the third listening.

LECTURE

↺

Follow-up: Take a minute to look at your notes. Do you see places where you missed information? Did you use key words as much as possible? Also check to see if the lecturer answered your prediction questions.

C. THIRD LISTENING

Use the third listening to check the notes you already have and to fill in any relevant details that you didn't have time to get down before.

LECTURE

↺

Follow-up: Keeping in mind that you will use your notes for a comprehensive quiz later on, check your notes with your teacher's or a classmate's. Do the two sets of notes have basically the same information? Do you believe that your notes are complete enough? Go on to the Accuracy Check before deciding if you need to listen to the lecture again.

3. Postlistening Activities

A. ACCURACY CHECK

Listen to the following statements. If a statement is true, put *T* in the space provided. If it is false, put *F*.

1. ______ 6. ______
2. ______ 7. ______
3. ______ 8. ______
4. ______ 9. ______
5. ______ 10. ______

Follow-up: Check your answers with your teacher. If you had less than 70% correct, you may need to listen to the lecture again and check the accuracy and completeness of your notes. (If possible, try to make arrangements to listen again outside class.)

B. ORAL PRACTICE

B.1. Review: Your teacher will ask different students to use their notes to give different parts of the lecture to the whole class. For example, Student A will give the introduction, Student B will discuss the first major subtopic, and so on. Following his or her own notes, each student who is listening should check the accuracy and completeness of his or her classmate's presentation.

Follow-up: Do you think your classmates left out any important information? If so, share your ideas with the class.

B.2. Transfer: Discuss with a partner the following questions:

1. What are the major religious groups in your country?
2. What is the relationship between the government and religion in your country?
3. Why do you think churches in the United States provide so many social activities and social services for their members?

C. HOMEWORK: READING COMPREHENSION

Read the following passage and answer the comprehension questions.

The Constitution and Religion

The issue of freedom of religion and separation of church and state has an interesting history. The First Amendment to the Constitution says, as follows:

> Congress shall make no law respecting an establishment of religion, or prohibiting the free exercise thereof; or abridging the freedom of speech, or of the press; or the right of the people peaceably to assemble and to petition the Government for a redress of grievances.

However, these rights were considered only a protection against interference by the *federal* government, and for more than a century the Supreme Court held that the *states* were not subject to the First Amendment and, therefore, states had a right to impose limitations on freedom of religion, speech, and the press. It wasn't until the 1920s that the Supreme Court began to change the way it made its decisions. At that time the Court began to use the Fourteenth Amendment (ratified in 1868), which says, in part;

> . . . nor shall any State deprive any person of life, liberty, or property, without due process of law. . . .

The Court argued that certain "fundamental rights" found in the Bill of Rights (the first ten amendments to the Constitution, all of which were passed by December 15, 1791) came under the meaning of liberty and therefore were protected by the "due process" clause.

Slowly, case by case, the Supreme Court ruled the First Amendment rights applicable to the states as well as to the federal government.

Comprehension Questions

1. What is the Bill of Rights?

____

____

2. By which time were all of the first ten amendments ratified?

____

____

3. How did the Supreme Court rule in cases where states limited freedom of religion, speech, and the press before the 1920s?

____

____

4. When was the Fourteenth Amendment ratified? What did it say, in part?

____

____

5. How did the Supreme Court use the Fourteenth Amendment to make the First Amendment rights applicable to the states as well as to the federal government?

____

____

Follow-up: Check your answers with your teacher.

CHAPTER 9

Passages: Birth, Marriage, and Death

1. Prelistening Activities

A. PREDICTIONS

Using the title of the lesson and the illustration as a starting point, share with your classmates what you already know or think about this topic. Then write three questions you think will be answered in this lecture.

1. ______________________________

2. ______________________________

3. ______________________________

Follow-up: After you have written your questions, share your questions with your teacher and your classmates.

B. VOCABULARY AND KEY CONCEPTS

Write the word or words you hear in the blanks provided in each sentence.

1. Customs and traditions are often ____________ to foreigners partly because the customs are so ____________ that people accept them without ever thinking about them.

2. The birth of a baby is a ____________ occasion in any family and is ____________ in some way.

3. The baby ____________ is given by a close friend or relative of the ____________ mother.

4. The ____________ is often invited to someone's home on some ____________ so that she can be surprised.

5. Gifts may be small ones depending on the financial situation of the ____________, but there is always a very emotional ____________ of good wishes for the coming baby.

6. Through advice and ____________ ____________, the expectant mother is ____________ about the desirability of her situation.

7. In the past men were ____________ from the ____________ room, but today many men are with their wives to "coach" them through the birth.

8. Christians usually have a religious service, called a ____________, for the new baby.

9. Some customs are generally ____________ concerning ____________, the engagement period, and the wedding ceremony.

10. Since priests, rabbis, and ministers are all legally ____________ to marry couples, it is not necessary to have both a ____________ and a religious ceremony.

11. Some customs about the ____________ and ____________ are rather ____________ in nature.

12. At the time of death, one decision is whether the funeral will be held in a church or in a funeral home; another decision is whether the body will be ____________ or buried in a cemetery.

13. The family may choose to have a ____________ service instead of a funeral. In either case, the family may hold a ____________, where the body of the deceased is displayed in a casket.

14. At a funeral, a ____________ is usually given by someone close to the ____________ person.

15. Those who want to express their ____________ usually send a sympathy card to the ____________ family.

Follow-up: Check the spelling of the dictated words with your teacher. Discuss the meanings of these words and any other unfamiliar words in the sentences.

C. NOTETAKING SKILLS

Key Words

We have already talked about using key words to save time and take good notes. Think of key words as a *telegram,* that is, the basic information in reduced form. Practice reducing the following sentences you will hear to key words. You will hear each sentence twice. Listen, decide on the key words, and write them in the space below. For example, as you listen to sentence 1, see how the author has used key words to reduce the information.

1. ethnic groups follow old customs, but *still* general culture in U.S.

Note: The notetaker here not only reduced the number of words in the sentence greatly but also reworded somewhat. Can *you* recreate the message of the sentence from these notes? Or would your notes look different?

Follow-up: Two students should write their key words on the board for other students to comment on and to compare theirs with. Keep in mind that good notes are notes which *you* can use to recall the ideas you heard.

2. Listening

A. FIRST LISTENING

The lecturer begins his talk with a discussion of cultural traditions in general, how the United States is somewhat different from many countries, and announces his subtopics: birth, marriage, and death. Since the subtopics consist of single words, you should be able to write down not only the subtopics but also some of the supporting details on the first listening.

LECTURE

NOTES

Introduction:

ST 1. ______________________________

ST 2. ______________________________

ST 3. ______________________________

Conclusion:

Follow-up: Were you able to use key words to take notes on at least two traditions related to each subtopic?

B. SECOND LISTENING

Continue using your key word strategy as you listen for additional relevant details to support the main subtopics. Once again leave space for additional information in the third listening. Also check to see if the lecturer answered your prediction questions.

LECTURE

Follow-up: Take a minute to look at your notes. Do you see places where you missed information? Did you use key words as much as possible?

C. THIRD LISTENING

Use the third listening to check the notes you already have and to fill in any relevant details that you didn't have time to get down before.

LECTURE

Follow-up: Keeping in mind that you will use your notes for a comprehensive quiz later on, check your notes with your teacher's or a classmate's. Do the two sets of notes have basically the same information? Do you believe that your notes are complete enough? Go on to the Accuracy Check before deciding if you need to listen to the lecture again.

3. Postlistening Activities

A. ACCURACY CHECK

Listen to the following statements. If a statement is true, put *T* in the space provided. If it is false, put *F*.

1. _____ 8. _____
2. _____ 9. _____
3. _____ 10. _____
4. _____ 11. _____
5. _____ 12. _____
6. _____ 13. _____
7. _____

Follow-up: Check your answers with your teacher. If you had fewer than nine correct, you may need to listen to the lecture again and check the accuracy and completeness of your notes. (If possible, try to make arrangements to listen again outside class.)

B. ORAL PRACTICE

B.1. Review: Working in pairs and using your notes, take turns giving parts of the lecture. Partner A should give the introduction and the first subtopic, and Partner B should discuss the second and third subtopic. Following his or her own notes, each student who is listening should check the accuracy and completeness of his or her partner's presentation.

Follow-up: How well were you and your partner able to reconstruct the lecture? Were you able to follow your partner? Were his or her notes complete enough?

B.2. Transfer: Choose *one* of the major subtopics (birth, marriage, or death) and carefully describe your customs related to this passage that differ from those in the United States. Your teacher may ask you to present your report orally to the class or to write a paragraph.

C. HOMEWORK: READING COMPREHENSION

Read the following passage and then answer the questions which follow about your society and culture.

Marriage Customs Around the World

There is certainly nothing unusual about marriage. People get married in virtually every society in the world. However, marriage is certainly not the same everywhere. In most cultures one man is expected to marry one woman, and the couple is expected to stay together until one of them dies or until they divorce. This style of marriage is called *monogamy*. However, in many cultures *polygamy* is practiced. In polygamy the man or the woman may have more than one spouse. Generally, it is the man who is allowed to take more than one wife. This arrangement is called *polygyny* and is practiced by many African and Middle Eastern peoples. A few societies permit *polyandry,* in which several men may marry one woman. In other words, polygamy can take two forms: polygyny and polyandry.

Another interesting aspect to marriage practices around the world is the question of who may marry whom in a culture. Sometimes a person is required to find a marriage partner *within* a certain group such as a tribe. This practice is called *endogamy.* Sometimes the most desirable marriage partner may be a first cousin. In other cases, a person must go *outside* a certain group and marry someone from a different family, tribe, or village. This practice is called *exogamy.* However, in virtually every society in the world there are strict rules against *incest,* that is, marrying certain family members such as a parent, a child, a brother, or a sister. This incest tabu is one of the few universal tabus in the world.

A third interesting difference which can be observed in different cultures around the world is the question of which family is expected to give gifts to the other family at the occasion of a marriage. Sometimes the bride's family is expected to give money or property to the bridegroom or his family. This is called a *dowry.* Sometimes this dowry is given directly to the bride who brings it to the marriage so that she and her groom may benefit from this money. In other societies the groom's family is expected to give property or money to the bride's family. This is called a *bride price.*

Comprehension Questions

1. Is your society monogamous or polygamous?

____

2. If your society is polygamous, do you practice polygyny or polyandry?

____

3. Does your society practice endogamy or exogamy?

____

4. Are you permitted to marry a first cousin in your society?

____

5. Does the bride's family give a dowry to the groom's family?

____

6. Does the bride's family give the bride a dowry to bring to the marriage?

____

7. Does the family of the groom give money or property to the family of the bride?

____

Follow-up: Check your answers with your teacher.

COMPREHENSIVE QUIZ DIRECTIONS

Now that you have completed from one to three chapters in this unit, your teacher may wish you to take a comprehensive quiz on the chapter or chapters which you have completed. Your teacher will tell you whether or not you can use your notes to answer the questions on this quiz. If you can use your notes, you should review them before taking the quiz so that you can anticipate the questions and know where to find the answers. If you cannot use your notes, *study them carefully before you take the quiz,* concentrating on organizing the information into main ideas and details which support these main ideas.

Before you begin writing your answers, read all the questions carefully. Your answers should be accurate and complete but brief. Do not include any information which does not answer the questions. You may have abbreviations in your notes, but do not use abbreviations in your answers. For those questions which are preceded by an asterisk, you must write your answers in complete sentences.

UNIT IV

Education

Schoolchildren on a field trip to a courthouse with their teacher.

C H A P T E R 1 0

Public Education: Philosophy and Funding

1. Prelistening Activities

A. PREDICTIONS

Using the title of the lesson and the illustration as a starting point, share with your classmates what you already know or think about this topic. Then write three questions you think will be answered in this lecture.

1. ____________________

2. ____________________

3. ____________________

Follow-up: After you have written your questions, share your questions with your teacher and your classmates.

B. VOCABULARY AND KEY CONCEPTS

Write the word or words you hear in the blanks provided in the following sentences.

1. Education in the United States is ____________ to a certain age or grade level.

2. A small percentage of students attend private schools, either religious or ____________, but most attend public schools.

3. Public education in the United States has ____________ that often surprise foreigners.

4. There is no ____________ ____________ or ____________ examinations set by the government.

5. The ____________ government influences public education by providing ____________ for special programs such as education for the ____________ and ____________ education.

6. Control of education in the United States is mainly ____________ ____________.

7. The state department of education ____________ basic curriculum requirements and the number of ____________ a high school student must have to graduate.

8. High school students take both required courses and ____________.

9. Each state has many school districts run by a school board whose members are ____________ by voters of the district.

10. One responsibility of the local school district is the ____________ of teachers and administrators.

11. Most funds for each school district come from residents in the district in the form of ____________.

12. There is an ______________ in the quality of education in different school districts, which results from the difference in taxes collected in richer and poorer districts.

Follow-up: Check the spelling of the dictated words with your teacher. Discuss the meanings of these words and any other unfamiliar words in the sentences.

C. NOTETAKING SKILLS

Structuring

A good notetaker will structure his or her notes as they are written to show the relative importance of ideas. Look at the following two sets of notes on a portion of this lecture.

Question 1: Which set is easier to read and use?
Question 2: Which set identified general ideas and more specific ones by their placement on the page?
Question 3: Which set of notes would be easier to study from for a quiz?

"The first level of control on education is the state department of education. The department of education of each of the fifty states has two basic functions. First, each state department of education sets certain basic curriculum requirements for all the schools in its state. For example, a high school might require four years of English, three years of math, two years of social science, and so forth. The state also sets the number of credits a student must complete in order to graduate from, for example, a high school. This total number of credits includes both required courses and electives. So much for the state part in education."

Set A: 1st level of control—state dept. of ed. 2 functions: curriculum req. 4 Eng, 3 math, 2 soc sci, for ex. and minimum credits to grad—req. & electives

Set B: 1st level of control—state dept of ed.
  2 functions
  curriculum req.
    4 Eng
    3 math
    2 soc sci, for ex.
  min. credits to grad
    req
    electives

Follow-up: A good notetaker makes an effort to structure his or her notes as in Set B above. Notice how the more general ideas appear to the left and the more specific ones to the right.

2. Listening

A. FIRST LISTENING

Listen for general ideas. After an introduction in which the lecturer mentions distinguishing features of public education in the United States, she goes on to discuss the three levels of control on education within each state which explain these features. She then goes on to explain how funding contributes to local control. As you listen, write down the four subtopics in the appropriate places.

LECTURE

NOTES

Introduction:

ST 1. ______________________________

ST 2. ______________________________

ST 3. ______________________________

ST 4. ______________________________

Follow-up: Check your major subtopics with your teacher before you listen to the lecture for the second time.

B. SECOND LISTENING

Use your structuring strategy as you listen for relevant details to support the main subtopics. Once again leave space for additional information in the third listening.

LECTURE

Follow-up: Take a minute to look at your notes. Do you see places where you missed information? Did you structure your notes so that you can distinguish important ideas from details? This would also be a good time to check to see if the lecturer has answered your prediction questions.

C. THIRD LISTENING

Use the third listening to check the notes you already have and to fill in any relevant details that you didn't have time to get down before.

LECTURE

Follow-up: Keeping in mind that you will use your notes for a comprehensive quiz later on, check your notes with your teacher's or a classmate's. Do the two sets of notes have basically the same information? Do you believe that your notes are complete enough? Go on to the Accuracy Check before deciding if you need to listen to the lecture again.

3. Postlistening Activities

A. ACCURACY CHECK

Listen to the following statements. If the statement is true, write *T* in the space provided. If the statement is false, write *F*.

1. ______ 6. ______
2. ______ 7. ______
3. ______ 8. ______
4. ______ 9. ______
5. ______ 10. ______

Follow-up: Check your answers with your teacher. If you had less than 70% correct, you may need to listen to the lecture again. (If possible, try to make arrangements to listen again outside class.)

B. ORAL PRACTICE

B.1. Review: Your teacher will ask different students to use their notes to give different parts of the lecture to the whole class. For example, Student A will give the introduction, Student B will discuss the first major subtopic, and so on. Following their own notes, the students who are listening should check the accuracy and completeness of their classmates' presentations.

Follow-up: Do you think your classmates left out any important information? If so, share your ideas with your class.

B.2. Transfer: Discuss and compare with a classmate how the educational system in your country is different from that in the United States. Try to use some of the ideas and vocabulary from

Vocabulary and Key Concepts, for example: *nationwide curriculum, standardized examinations, required courses, electives, funding, control, compulsory*. Discuss how the systems are similar and how they are different.

Follow-up: Were you able to discuss and compare the different educational systems? If you and your classmates are from different countries, did you learn something new about the educational system of your classmate's country? Were you able to ask him or her the questions that you wanted to? If so, you were both successful.

C. HOMEWORK: VOCABULARY REVIEW

Fill in the blanks with a word from the following list. Some words will be used twice. The following is a summary of the lecture you heard.

administrators	bilingual	board
compulsory	course	credits
curriculum	elected	electives
feature	federal	funds
handicapped	hiring	how
inequity	local	nationwide
prepare	private	public
secular	standardized	taxes

Public Education in the United States

Generally speaking, education in the United States is ____________ and ____________ although a few students attend either religious or ____________ ____________ schools. One ____________ which distinguishes the American public schools from many others is that the government does not determine a ____________ ____________. Moreover, the government does not set ____________ examinations. In contrast to many educational systems around the world, control of education in the States is largely at the ____________ level. However, the federal government does exercise some control by the way it provides ____________ for special educational programs, such as programs for ____________ people or for ____________ education.

The state department of education in each state determines the basic ____________ and the number of ____________ a student must have in order to graduate. Students take required courses, but they can also take ____________ which particularly interest them. Local school districts are run by a school ____________. People on the school board are ____________ by local citizens. School boards are responsible for ____________ content, which ____________ are offered, and for the ____________ of teachers and ____________. ____________ the content of each course is taught is the responsibility of the teachers of each school itself. Teachers also ____________ and give examinations to the students.

The largest percentage of funds for schools come from taxes raised in the ____________ school district—about 53%. The second largest amount—about 40%—comes from state ____________, and the smallest percentage—about 7%—comes from the ____________ government. There is an ____________ in the education in poor and rich communities because of the difference in the amount of taxes which can be raised for education.

Follow-up: Check your answers with your teacher.

CHAPTER 11

Postsecondary Education: Admissions*

1. Prelistening Activities

A. PREDICTIONS

Using the title of the lesson and the illustration as a starting point, share with your classmates what you already know or think about this topic. Then write three questions you think will be answered in this lecture.

1. ______________________________

2. ______________________________

3. ______________________________

Follow-up: After you have written your questions, share your questions with your teacher and your classmates.

*For those of you who would like to or plan to attend an American college or university, we would like to refer you to the Foreign Student Information Clearinghouse, which publishes a very useful free booklet. This booklet gives you some general information about the numbers of schools which accept foreign students and tells you how to find out which schools might be suitable to your needs and abilities. Write to this address for a booklet: The Foreign Student Information Clearinghouse, 888 Seventh Avenue, New York, NY 10106, USA.

B. VOCABULARY AND KEY CONCEPTS

Write the word or words you hear in the blanks provided in the following sentences.

1. ____________ education in the United States includes ____________ as well as senior colleges, most of which are ____________ .

2. To be ____________, a college must meet certain ____________ set by institutional and professional associations.

3. The more ____________ private schools are more ____________, that is, they have stiffer admissions requirements.

4. All college applicants must submit a ____________ of high school grades and often ____________ test results.

5. A student's ____________ activities and possibly his ____________ ____________ are often factors in his admission.

6. Some freshmen ____________ ____________ of school after their first year rather than ____________ for a second year.

7. Some students begin college at a junior college with more ____________ admissions requirements and later ____________ to a senior college.

Follow-up: Check the spelling of the dictated words with your teacher. Discuss the meanings of these words and any other unfamiliar words in the sentences.

C. NOTETAKING SKILLS

Structuring

In the previous lesson we talked about *structuring* notes to make them clearer and easier to use. Practice structuring your notes as you *listen* to a portion of this lecture. Remember to move from left to right as you take down more specific information. The main idea, the most general one, is written for you. An outline is provided to guide you. You'll hear this section of the lecture two times.

ST 3. Junior colleges differ from sen. colls.
A.
  1.
B.
  1.
  2.
C.
  1.
  2.
Conclusion:

Follow-up: Compare your notes with your teacher's or another student's. Do you have the same information under A, B, and C?

Culturegram: Many terms and long names are commonly written and spoken in their abbreviated form in English. *U.S.* and *U.N.* are common abbreviations using the first letter of each word. In this lecture the following tests and degrees will be referred to in abbreviated form. As you write the first-letter abbreviations, say them to yourself. When you take notes, use the abbreviations.

Graduate Record Examination	G.R.E.
Graduate Management Admissions Test	________________
Law School Admission Test	________________
Medical College Admission Test	________________
Scholastic Aptitude Test	________________
Associate of Arts degree	A.A. degree

Bachelor of Science degree ____________

Bachelor of Arts degree ____________

2. Listening

A. FIRST LISTENING

The lecturer appears to be in a hurry today to get into her topic. Her introduction is very brief and basically consists of an announcement of her three major subtopics. You will not need to take notes on the introduction itself. However, notice as you listen that the conclusion, which begins with "in brief," contains important logical conclusions about the three subtopics that you will want to include in your notes.

Important: Beginning with this lecture, you will hear the lecture *two* times only. Therefore, you will need to get not only major subtopics on the first listening, but also as many relevant supporting details as possible. (Remember that you already have ST 3 with supporting details from the Notetaking Skills exercise.)

LECTURE

NOTES

ST 1. ____________________________

ST 2. ______________________________

ST 3. ______________________________

Conclusion:

Follow-up: Were you able to hear when the lecturer changed from one main topic to the next? Check your major subtopics with your teacher. Which subtopic would you look under to answer the following questions?

1. What are two factors a college or university might use to decide whether or not to admit a student?
2. What is the range (from low to high) of the total cost of attending a college or university?
3. Where can you receive an Associate of Arts degree?

B. SECOND (FINAL) LISTENING

Did you have the answers to these questions in your notes? During the second listening, try to get down the remaining relevant details. (*Note:* We will not remind you to check prediction questions in future lessons.)

LECTURE

Follow-up: Keeping in mind that you will use your notes later for a comprehensive quiz, compare your notes with your teacher's or your classmates'.

3. Postlistening Activities

A. ACCURACY CHECK

For numbers 1–4 listen to the following questions and circle the letter of the best answer.

1. a. 300
   b. 1,300
   c. 3,000
   d. 13,000
2. a. a transcript of his grade
   b. MACT score
   c. SAT score
   d. extracurricular activities
3. a. one fifth
   b. one fourth
   c. one third
   d. one half

4. Junior colleges ______.
   a. are cheaper to go to
   b. are easier to be admitted to
   c. offer vocational education
   d. don't offer a degree

For numbers 5–10 listen to the following statements. If the statement is true, put *T* next to the correct number. If the statement is false, put *F*.

5. ______ 8. ______
6. ______ 9. ______
7. ______ 10. ______

Follow-up: Check your answers with your teacher. If you had less than 70% correct, you may need to listen to the lecture again. (If possible, try to make arrangements to listen again outside class.)

B. ORAL PRACTICE

B.1. Review: Your teacher will ask different students to use their notes to give different parts of the lecture to the whole class. Student A will discuss the first major subtopic. Student B will discuss the second major subtopic, and so on. Following their own notes, the students who are listening should check the accuracy and completeness of their classmates' presentations.

Follow-up: Do you think your classmates left out any important information? If so, share your ideas with your class.

B.2. Transfer: Discuss the following questions with a partner if you are from different countries or with your teacher if you are from the same country:

How many colleges and universities are there in your country?
What kinds of colleges and universities do you have?
Where are these schools located—in major cities and/or small towns?
Approximately how many students are there at these schools?
What percentage of high school graduates go on to a university?

More Discussion: Some countries take a more elitist approach to education than does the United States. That is, some countries consciously limit the number of students who can go on to college by means of a highly competitive examination system. With your partner or your teacher discuss the following two questions:

1. What might be some of the social, political, and economic reasons for an elitist educational system?
2. What are the advantages and disadvantages of the two different approaches to education—elitist and non-elitist?

C. HOMEWORK: READING

The following reading describes the public education system in the United States from kindergarten through high school. As you read, think about the similarities to the system in your country and the dissimilarities. Make notes in the space which follows the reading under the correct heading. Don't write sentences—just make notes. For example, perhaps children start school at age seven in your country, or perhaps they begin at age four. If so, make a note of the difference. Example: Under United States—begin at five; under Your Country—begin at seven (or four).

Public Education in the United States

The public education system in the United States is difficult to describe at times. There is no nationwide standardized curriculum. Nor are there standardized nationwide or even statewide exams that all students take. Each state determines the general curriculum for its schools, but there is still variety from school to school, and not all students within the same high school will take the same courses. Although it's difficult to generalize about education in the States, there are, of course, *some* general things that can be said about it.

A natural place to begin is with the elementary school years. Although most states require children to be in school by the age of six, most youngsters attend kindergarten at age five. This first year of school, kindergarten, is a period of socialization and of preparation to learn in future years. At age six most children attend first grade. The majority of children will remain in the public school system for twelve years: six years of elementary school, two or three years of junior high school, and three or four years of high school. When students enter public high school, they have little choice of which school they will attend or which courses they will take. As they did for elementary and junior high school, they attend the nearest school located in the school district they live in. After the first year of high school, they can elect certain courses in addition to courses required for graduation. Most high schools offer a comprehensive education. This means that students may choose to specialize in an academic, a general, or a vocational course of study at the same school. Specialized high schools which train only craftsmen and tradesmen, or only scientists, for example, are virtually nonexistent in the United States. The educational philosophy of public schools is to give every student a general education while at the same time to allow some individual choice of courses which students feel will be relevant to their futures.

Entrance to one's local high school is automatic, assuming that a student has finished junior high school successfully. There is no entrance exam for high school.

To graduate from high school, students must satisfy the school's minimum requirements of courses and grade point average. For example, a particular high school might require four years of English, three years of math, two years of science, one or two years of a foreign language, and two social studies courses. Once again, there is no nationwide examination which all high school students are required to pass in order to graduate. With no standardized high-school exams prepared by a Ministry of Education or a Department of Education, you may wonder how students are admitted to universities. Actually there *are* standardized nationwide exams which many high school students take, especially those students who plan to go on to college or a university. However, these exams are not prepared by the school system, and they are only one of several factors which colleges and universities look at in deciding which students to admit. You will hear more about these exams in your next lecture.

Your Country	*United States*

Follow-up: Discuss the similarities and differences with your classmates and your teacher.

CHAPTER 12

University Life

1. Prelistening Activities

A. PREDICTIONS

Using the title of the lesson and the illustration as a starting point, share with your classmates what you already know or think about this topic. Then write three questions you think will be answered in this lecture.

1. ______________________________

2. ______________________________

3. ______________________________

Follow-up: After you have written your questions, share your questions with your teacher and your classmates.

B. VOCABULARY AND KEY CONCEPTS

Write the word or words you hear in the blanks provided in the following sentences.

1. The student body on a U.S. campus is diverse; one meets students of greatly different ages, from different racial and ____________ ____________, and from different ____________ levels.

2. Let's begin by talking about an ____________ student entering his or her ____________ year.

3. Foreign students often find U.S. students less well-prepared for college than they expected. The U.S. students are often not very ____________ - ____________ in international matters or very ____________ - ____________ about foreign countries.

4. To ____________ how the average U.S. university class might be different, it will be helpful to begin by discussing the ____________ .

5. ____________ dates of assignments, dates of exams, and the teacher's ____________ ____________ are usually all found on the course syllabus.

6. A major difference in graduate school is that some classes are conducted as ____________ without exams and quizzes. This is only possible with highly ____________ and ____________ students, of course.

Follow-up: Check the spelling of the dictated words with your teacher. Discuss the meanings of these words and any other unfamiliar words in the sentences.

C. NOTETAKING SKILLS

Rhetorical Cues

One of the most important notetaking skills is the ability to recognize those rhetorical cues, or signals, which indicate that the speaker is about to introduce or change a topic. Here are some common ways a speaker uses to signal these changes:

I'd like to take a few minutes . . .
Let's begin by . . .
Let's move on now . . .
I have only a couple of minutes left . . . (This will come close to the end of the lecture, but it usually doesn't signal a conclusion. It usually means the introduction of a final topic to be discussed.)

Another device used by speakers to introduce a new topic is the rhetorical question. A rhetorical question is one that is not meant to be answered. The speaker uses it to open a topic. You will hear this rhetorical question in the lecture: What kind of university experiences will this so-called "average" student have?

Culturegram: In this lecture you will hear the following words all used interchangeably to mean postsecondary education: college, university, school. The lecturer will use "high school" when she is referring to secondary school. Otherwise she is talking about postsecondary education.

2. Listening

A. FIRST LISTENING

The lecturer begins with an introduction about the diversity of the student body at a typical American university or college. Listen for the signals you read about to help you recognize when the lecturer is about to change to another major subtopic. Write down the main subtopics and as many of the relevant supporting details as possible.

LECTURE

NOTES

Introduction:

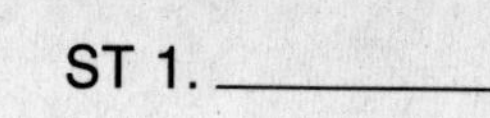

ST 1. ________________________________

ST 2. ________________________________

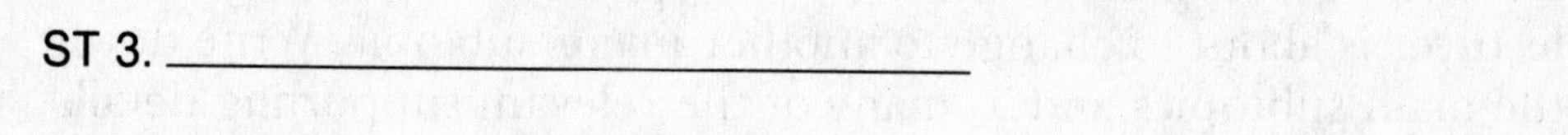

ST 3. ________________________________

ST 4. ______________________

Follow-up: Did listening for the lecturer's signals that she was about to introduce or change a topic help you identify the main subtopics? Check your major subtopics with your teacher.

B. SECOND (FINAL) LISTENING

Try to write down as many more relevant details as possible during the second listening.

LECTURE

Follow-up: Keeping in mind that you will use your notes later for a comprehensive quiz, compare your notes with your teacher's or your classmates'.

3. Postlistening Activities

A. ACCURACY CHECK

For numbers 1–5 listen to the following statements. If the statement is true, write *T* in the space provided. If the statement is false, write *F*.

1. _____
2. _____
3. _____
4. _____
5. _____

For numbers 6–9 listen to the following questions and circle the letter of the best answer.

6. a. U.S. high school students don't study world geography and history.
   b. Foreign universities are less selective than U.S. ones.
   c. A larger proportion of young people go to college in the United States than in many other countries.
   d. U.S. students are of diverse ages and ethnic backgrounds.
7. a. Many of his classes will be very large lecture classes.
   b. He has a chance to ask questions and clarify points from lectures in small discussion groups.
   c. His English and German classes won't generally have many students in them.
   d. He spends a lot of time reviewing class notes and very little time preparing for class.
8. a. how students should dress for the class
   b. what the students will study
   c. when assignments must be handed in
   d. what material the exams will cover
9. In contrast to undergraduate students, graduate students are expected to ______ .
   a. read to prepare for class
   b. write papers
   c. do more independent work
   d. attend class regularly

Follow-up: Check your answers with your teacher. If you had fewer than 7 out of 9 answers correct, you may need to listen to the lecture again. (If possible, try to make arrangements to listen again outside class.)

B. ORAL PRACTICE

B.1. Review: Use your notes and take turns giving different sections of the lecture to the class. Student A will give the introduction, Student B will give the first subtopic, and so on. While your classmates are speaking, follow your notes and check on the accuracy and completeness of their presentations.

Follow-up: Were your classmates able to talk about how university life in the United States is different from that in many other countries? If you noticed any inaccuracies or important omissions, discuss these with your classmates.

B.2. Transfer: Discuss with a partner or with the class what information an American student attending a university in your country would need to know.

How is your student body different from the student body in the United States?
What is an "average" student in your country like?
What is an "average" class like?
How is the examination system different?
How do professors in your country conduct their classes?
How is graduate school different from undergraduate school?

C. HOMEWORK: DECIPHERING NOTES

Imagine that you missed a lecture in which your professor discussed some basic differences between U.S. colleges and universities and those in foreign countries which were not discussed in the lecture in this lesson. Because you were absent, you photocopied a classmate's notes. See if you can use these notes to answer your teacher's questions. Work with a partner if possible.

Educ. System in Coll. or Univ.

1. Kinds of courses
   a. required [sometimes choice among some required courses = alternatives]
   b. elective – students choose
   c. pre-requisite – required before another course can be taken

2. Schedule
   - very flexible
   - late afternoon / evening courses (working students)

3. Classes
   - different people class to class
   - great variety of kinds of people
   } => difficult for some young freshmen from small homogeneous high schools, big change

Directions: Answer in complete sentences.

1. What are *prerequisites*?

____

____

2. What is the difference between an alternative class and an elective class?

____

____

3. Why are the same classes sometimes offered both during the day and in the late afternoon or evening?

____

____

4. Why do incoming freshmen from small high schools sometimes suffer from a kind of culture shock?

____

____

Follow-up: Check your answers with your teacher.

COMPREHENSIVE QUIZ DIRECTIONS

Now that you have completed from one to three chapters in this unit, your teacher may wish you to take a comprehensive quiz on the chapter or chapters which you have completed. Your teacher will tell you whether or not you can use your notes to answer the questions on this quiz. If you can use your notes, you should review them before taking the quiz so that you can anticipate the questions and know where to find the answers. If you cannot use your notes, *study them carefully before you take the quiz,* concentrating on organizing the information into main ideas and details which support these main ideas.

Before you begin writing your answers, read all the questions carefully. Your answers should be accurate and complete but brief. Do not include any information which does not answer the questions. You may have abbreviations in your notes, but do not use abbreviations in your answers. For those questions which are preceded by an asterisk, you must write your answers in complete sentences.

UNIT V

Economy

CHAPTER 13

The Economy at Home and in the World

1. Prelistening Activities

A. PREDICTIONS

Using the title of the lesson and the illustration as a starting point, share with your classmates what you already know or think about this topic. Then write three questions you think will be answered in this lecture.

1. ______________________________

2. ______________________________

3. ______________________________

Follow-up: After you have written your questions, share your questions with your teacher and your classmates.

B. VOCABULARY AND KEY CONCEPTS

Write the word or words you hear in the blanks provided in the following sentences.

1. With a small percentage of the world __________ __________, the United States produces a rather large

percentage of the world's total ______________ ______________ ______________.

2. We'll take a closer look at the makeup of the U.S. labor force in terms of how many people are ______________ in different ______________ of the economy.

3. The United States has an ______________ on other countries through imports and exports as well as through ______________ made by U.S. businesses abroad.

4. Two factors contributing to the United States' economic power are a ______________ labor force and vast supplies of ______________ ______________.

5. In the 1970s the ______________ ______________ ______________ of the United States was greater than that of the Common Market countries taken together.

6. Three important sectors of the U.S. economy are ______________, the ______________ sector, and retail and wholesale ______________.

7. The figures for the ______________ ______________ are much lower but higher than those for agriculture, ______________, and fishing.

8. When a country has ______________ ______________ ______________ problems, the solution often lies in arrangements with the countries leading ______________ partners.

9. Both ______________ and ______________ rates can be reasons for a balance of trade problem, and ______________ trade laws are sometimes used as a solution.

Follow-up: Check the spelling of the dictated words with your teacher. Discuss the meanings of these words and any other unfamiliar words in the sentences.

C. NOTETAKING SKILLS

Recognizing Relevant Information

In this lecture the lecturer discusses the U.S. economy in a world perspective. In doing so, the lecturer conveys a lot of information quickly. Since he makes a point of announcing "*two* reasons for the strength of the U.S. economy," the *six* sectors of the economy, and the United States' *five* major trading partners, be prepared to get all the parts of each category down in your notes. Since the lecturer is giving *complete,* exhaustive lists rather than just a few examples, we recognize this information as relevant and noteworthy. Therefore, when you hear "six sectors," you should quickly write a list like this in your notes in order to have a place to write the information you will hear:

Sectors
1.
2.
3.
etc.

2. Listening

A. FIRST LISTENING

The lecturer begins with a little anecdote illustrating the economic impact of the United States on the world. This type of story is *not* noteworthy. However, the pace changes quickly, and you will need to write down the major subtopics and as many relevant details as quickly as possible.

LECTURE

NOTES

ST 1. ______________________________

ST 2. ______________________________

ST 3. ______________________________

ST 4. ______________________________

Follow-up: Check your major subtopics with your teacher before you listen to the lecture for the second time. Were you able to number the lists and at least partially complete them on the first listening?

B. SECOND (FINAL) LISTENING

Check the notes you have and fill in information you missed on the first listening.

LECTURE

Follow-up: Keeping in mind that you will use your notes for a comprehensive quiz later on, check your notes with your teacher's or a classmate's.

3. Postlistening Activities

A. ACCURACY CHECK

Listen to the following questions and circle the letter of the best answer.

1. The United States ______.
   a. work force is about 6% of the world's total population
   b. produces about 25% of the world's total output of goods
   c. imports about 10% of its needs
   d. imports little because it is self-sufficient
2. a. a large labor force and membership in the Common market
   b. many vocational schools and a good transportation system
   c. well-trained labor force and great natural resources
   d. a growing service sector and lots of doctors and lawyers
3. a. $4,000,000
   b. $4,000,000,000
   c. $4,000,000,000,000
   d. $4,000,000,000,000,000
4. the total value of ______
   a. exports
   b. exports and imports
   c. its industrial output
   d. the goods and services it produces
5. a. service
   b. manufacturing
   c. commerce
   d. agriculture
6. a. chemicals
   b. corn and soybeans
   c. transportation equipment
   d. non-electrical machines
7. a. manufacturing a car
   b. exporting petroleum
   c. visiting a doctor
   d. washing someone's car for money
8. a. Mexico
   b. East Germany
   c. Britain
   d. Canada

9. A negative balance of trade ________.
   a. is a favorable situation for a country
   b. happens when a country exports more than it imports
   c. is directly tied to restrictive trade laws
   d. none of the above
10. a. He doesn't want to trade with the United States.
   b. The United States tries to harm its neighbors economically.
   c. The United States affects neighboring countries greatly.
   d. The United States is difficult to understand.

Follow-up: Check your answers with your teacher. If you had less than 70% correct, you may need to listen to the lecture again. (If possible, try to make arrangements to listen again outside class.)

B. ORAL PRACTICE

B.1. Review: Your teacher will ask different students to use their notes to give different parts of the lecture to the whole class. For example, Student A will discuss the first major subtopic, Student B the second subtopic, and so on. The students who are listening should check the accuracy and completeness of their classmates' presentations.

Follow-up: Do you think your classmates left out any important information? If so, share your ideas with your class.

B.2. Transfer: Using the vocabulary and concepts in this lesson, prepare six questions that you could use to interview a person from another country about the economy of his or her country.

Example: How does your country fit into the global economic picture?

1. ________________________________

2. ________________________________

3. ________________________________

4. ________________________________

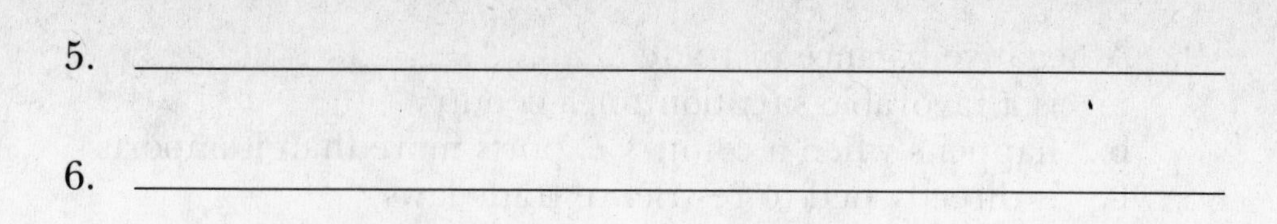

5. ______________________________

6. ______________________________

Follow-up: If possible, interview a person from another country. If this is not possible, use the questions to practice language with another student from your country.

C. HOMEWORK: VOCABULARY REVIEW

Use the following words to complete the passage. Use each word one time.

balance · chemicals · exports
fishing · imports · industrialized
manufacturing · produced · resources
sector · trading

The Economy of Switzerland

It might be interesting to look at the economy of Switzerland, which, with very different conditions from those in the United States, has been a very successful country economically with one of the highest standards of living in the world. There are actually more jobs than the Swiss themselves can fill and a large number of foreign workers have come from other countries to work there.

Unlike the United States, Switzerland has few natural ____________. The three most important are water power, timber, and salt. The water power, provided by Switzerland's swift-moving mountain rivers, is probably her most important resource. The hydroelectric power stations on these rivers provide most of the electric power ____________ in the country, and its wide distribution allows factories to be distributed widely throughout the country. This relatively small West-European country is one of the most highly ____________ countries in the world. It's no surprise then that 32% of the economy is based on ____________. The service ____________ represents 28% of economic activity, and commerce represents 19%. Agriculture, forestry, and ____________ contribute about 7% to the GNP.

Switzerland's GNP in 1985 was well over one hundred billion dollars. Her major ____________ partners were West Germany, France, Italy, Britain, and the United States. Unlike the United States, Switzerland in recent years has had more ____________ than imports. Therefore, the country is not bothered by a negative trade ____________ . As we might expect, raw materials such as iron, steel and fuel are among Switzerland's ____________ . Exports, besides the clocks and watches everyone knows, include textiles, ____________, and dyestuffs.

Follow-up: Check your answers with your teacher.

New York Stock Exchange.

CHAPTER 14

Capitalism U.S. Style

1. Prelistening Activities

A. PREDICTIONS

Using the title of the lesson and the illustration as a starting point, share with your classmates what you already know or think about this topic. Then write three questions you think will be answered in this lecture.

1. ______________________________

2. ______________________________

3. ______________________________

Follow-up: After you have written your questions, share your questions with your teacher and your classmates.

B. VOCABULARY AND KEY CONCEPTS

Write the word or words you hear in the blanks provided in the following sentences.

1. The Soviet Union is closer to the purely ____________ type of economy while the United States is closer to the purely ____________ type.

2. As a mostly capitalist country, the United States is a ____________ ____________, which means that private business people, not the government, decide what to produce, how much to produce, and what price to sell the products for.

3. In a socialist system, economic decisions are made by the ____________ ____________ ____________ of the government.

4. Business people, who are motivated by a desire for ____________, decide what goods and services to produce.

5. Simply put, the interaction of ____________ and ____________ determines the prices of goods and services in the capitalist market.

6. A characteristic of U.S. capitalism is ____________ ____________ of property.

7. Since the capitalist system also recognizes the products of intellectual activity as private property, there are ____________ laws to protect books and ____________ laws to protect inventions.

8. Another cornerstone of the U.S. economy is ____________ ____________, which allows for the buying and selling of goods without government ____________ .

9. Free ____________ ____________ ensure that neither buyers nor sellers will control the market.

10. In a competitive system, a certain number of business ____________ and ____________ are normal.

Follow-up: Check the spelling of the dictated words with your teacher. Discuss the meanings of these words and any other unfamiliar words in the sentences.

C. NOTETAKING SKILLS

Structuring: Comparison

The lecturer begins by telling you that there are two main types of economic systems, socialist and capitalist. He then tells you the major differences between the systems. He concludes the discussion by giving examples of countries which are closer to one system or the other. When you are taking notes, it's useful to try to anticipate organization and to structure your major heading and subheadings according to the organization. For a comparison the speaker should mention the same points for each person, place, or thing he is comparing. Therefore, you need to leave space under each topic for similar information. When taking notes, it's also a good idea to space your main subtopics and their subtopics to leave enough room for details. Listen to the first major subtopic and decide which of the following outlines better represents the structure of this part of the lecture.

PLAN A:

Subtopic 1. Differences between Capitalism and Socialism

A. Resources
    1. Socialism
    2. Capitalism
B. Decisions
    1. Cap.
    2. Soc.
C. Examples
    1. Cap.
    2. Soc.

PLAN B:

Subtopic 1. Differences between Capitalism and Socialism

A. Resources in Socialism
B. Decisions in Soc.
C. Resources and Decisions in Capitalism
D. Examples of Soc.
E. Examples of Cap.

Follow-up: After discussing with your teacher and classmates which of the two possible outlines would be more useful, copy the outline (subtopic and the supporting details) onto your notetaking page under Subtopic 1. Don't forget to leave space for the notes you might add when you listen a second time.

2. Listening

A. FIRST LISTENING

You already know what the first major subtopic is. There is one other major subtopic. As you listen to the lecture and take notes, notice that the second subtopic basically consists of economic terms and their definitions. These definitions are not just a few words to explain a new term. Rather they are quite long and consist of examples and illustrations to help you understand these new terms.

LECTURE

NOTES

ST 1. ______________________________

ST 2. ______________________________

Follow-up: Check your major subtopics with your teacher before you listen to the lecture for the second time.

B. SECOND (FINAL) LISTENING

Check the notes you have and fill in any information you missed on the first listening.

LECTURE

Follow-up: Keeping in mind that you will use your notes for a comprehensive quiz later on, check your notes with your teacher's or a classmate's.

3. Postlistening Activities

A. ACCURACY CHECK

For numbers 1–5 write *T* if the statement is true and *F* if the statement is false.

1. _____
2. _____
3. _____
4. _____
5. _____

For numbers 6–10 listen to the question and circle the letter of the best answer.

6. a. Switzerland
   b. the People's Republic of China
   c. Hong Kong
   d. the United States
7. a. a house
   b. a book
   c. a bankruptcy
   d. an invention
8. a. the government
   b. consumers
   c. producers
   d. both b and c
   e. both a and c
9. a. There are lots of buyers and sellers.
   b. A small group of sellers does not control the market.
   c. Not all businesses will succeed in the market.
   d. all of the above
   e. none of the above
10. a. central planning agency
    b. individual ownership of property
    c. free enterprise
    d. free competitive markets

Follow-up: Check your answers with your teacher. If you had less than 70% correct, you may need to listen to the lecture again and check the accuracy and completeness of your notes. (If possible, try to make arrangements to listen again outside class.)

B. ORAL PRACTICE

B.1. Review: Working in pairs, use your notes to practice giving sections of the lecture to each other. Student A will present the introduction and the first subtopic and its details to Student B. Student B will present the second and third major subtopics and their details to Student A. Following his or her own notes, the student who is listening should check the accuracy and completeness of his or her partner's presentation.

Follow-up: Were your notes complete and accurate enough for you to do this oral practice activity with relative ease? Did you and your partner agree on essential information? If not, you may need to listen to the lecture again.

B.2. Transfer: With a partner or as a class discuss the advantages and disadvantages of both major economic systems: capitalism and socialism.

C. HOMEWORK: READING COMPREHENSION

Read the following passage and answer the questions.

The Moroccan Bazaar

We have talked at length about the American market economy. It might be interesting to look at another type of economy and see how the market works. One economy we can look at is the bazaar economy of Morocco. Bazaars (*suqs* in Arabic) are real marketplaces, some of which are in permanent locations and others of which exist for certain periods of times. For a typical tourist the bazaar can be a noisy, colorful, confusing place which appears to have no order. Everything from bolts of cloth to cattle, from dates to cooking utensils are for sale. There are no fixed prices. Every business transaction must be negotiated with the buyer and the seller agreeing on the price at the time of the actual sale.

What are some of the characteristics of the bazaar economy? First, as in most market economies, most artisans do not sell the products that they make. These products are sold by shopkeepers who often specialize in one kind of item, such as rugs, or a few items in the same category, such as leather goods. Another characteristic of the bazaar is that activities inside the bazaar are highly competitive, and ways to keep down costs of doing business have been developed. One of these ways to keep down the cost of making business transactions is to have professional auctioneers who help to keep transactions moving quickly. Another way is to have a group of specialized brokers. These brokers go from bazaar to bazaar, buying goods cheaply at one bazaar and reselling them for a profit at another bazaar. A final characteristic of the bazaar is that it is unregulated. There is no government intervention. Disputes are rare because in this highly competitive atmosphere a reputation for honesty is one of the most important assets a shopkeeper can have. The occasional dispute which does arise is settled by private arbitrators (people who specialize in settling disputes). The bazaar seems to function quite smoothly overall, noisily, perhaps, but smoothly.

Adapted from "Exchange in the Bazaar Economy," in *Microeconomics,* second edition, Robert B. Ekelund, Jr. and Robert D. Tollison, Scott, Foresman, and Company: Boston, 1988, pp. 73–74.

Comprehension Questions

1. How is the Moroccan bazaar different from a modern department store in terms of items sold and the prices of items?
2. What is the difference between an "artisan" and a "shopkeeper" in this context?
3. What are two ways of keeping down the cost of doing business in the Moroccan bazaar?
4. If there is no government regulation or intervention in the bazaar, how is it that disputes seldom occur?

Follow-up: Check your answers with your teacher.

Three Mile Island—nuclear reactors.

CHAPTER 15

The Role of Government in the Economy

1. Prelistening Activities

A. PREDICTIONS

Using the title of the lesson and the illustration as a starting point, share with your classmates what you already know or think about this topic. Then write three questions you think will be answered in this lecture.

1. ______________________________

2. ______________________________

3. ______________________________

Follow-up: After you have written your questions, share your questions with your teacher and your classmates.

B. VOCABULARY AND KEY CONCEPTS

Write the word or words you hear in the blanks provided in the following sentences.

1. In a pure capitalistic system, the government's role is severely limited. It would be responsibile only for laws governing

_____________ and property, as well as for the _____________ _____________.

2. The idea in a pure capitalistic system is for the government not to _____________, that is, for the government to take a _____________ - _____________ attitude.

3. Companies may have to install pollution _____________ equipment to _____________ _____________ government regulations.

4. People who earn little or no _____________ can receive _____________ _____________, often called _____________.

5. The government makes sure the market place stays _____________ through its _____________ and _____________ laws.

6. The government interferes with the economy in an effort to maintain _____________.

7. Through _____________ the government tries to control _____________.

8. The government has to be very careful to keep _____________ and inflation in _____________, however.

9. The government further tries to achieve stability through its _____________ and by controlling the _____________ rate.

Follow-up: Check the spelling of the dictated words with your teacher. Discuss the meanings of these words and any other unfamiliar words in the sentences.

C. NOTETAKING SKILLS

Structuring: Classification

In this rather sophisticated lecture, the subtopics grow progressively more complex. Subtopic 4 itself is broken into different methods that the government uses to maintain economic stability, which the lecturer mentions initially and then goes on to discuss in detail. Listen to this portion of the lecture one time and choose which of the following two partial outlines best represents the structure of subtopic 4.

PLAN A:

Subtopic 4. Government interferes to maintain economic stability.

A.
B.
C.
  1.
  2.

PLAN B:

Subtopic 4. Government interferes to maintain economic stability.

A.
B.
C.
D.
  1.
  2.
E.
  1.
  2.
F.
  1.
  2.

Follow-up: Which outline did you and your classmates choose? Why? After discussing this with your teacher, use the correct outline form under subtopic 4 when you take notes.

2. Listening

A. FIRST LISTENING

In the introduction the lecturer discusses how a *pure* capitalist government would function in order to point out how the United States is *not* a pure capitalist country, and then he goes on to explain *why* the government interferes. Notice that the lecturer starts out with the simpler reasons and finishes with the most complex.

LECTURE

NOTES

Introduction:

ST 1. ________________________________

ST 2. ______________________________

ST 3. ______________________________

ST 4. ______________________________

Follow-up: Check your major subtopics with your teacher before you listen to the lecture for the second time.

B. SECOND (FINAL) LISTENING

Check the notes you have and fill in any information that you missed on the first listening.

LECTURE

Follow-up: Keeping in mind that you will use your notes for a comprehensive quiz later on, check your notes with your teacher's or a classmate's.

3. Postlistening Activities

A. ACCURACY CHECK

Listen to the following statements. If the statement is true, put *T* in the space provided. If it is false, put *F*.

1. ______ 6. ______
2. ______ 7. ______
3. ______ 8. ______
4. ______ 9. ______
5. ______ 10. ______

Follow-up: Check your answers with your teacher. If you had less than 70% correct, you may need to listen to the lecture again and check the accuracy and completeness of your notes. (If possible, try to make arrangements to listen again outside class.)

B. ORAL PRACTICE

B.1. Review: Your teacher will ask different students to use their notes to give different parts of the lecture to the whole class. For example, Student A will give the introduction, Student B will discuss the first major subtopic, and so on. The students who are listening should check the accuracy and completeness of their classmates' presentations.

Follow-up: Do you think your classmates left out any important information? If so, share your ideas with your class.

B.2. Transfer: As a class discuss the following questions. Give your opinions about what you believe a good government should be like.

1. Should the role of government be limited to national defense, making laws concerning property and contracts, and the building of roads? Why or why not?
2. Should the role of government in the economy be limited or should the government take an active role?
3. Many people believe that government help to people makes these people lazy. Do you agree? Why or why not?

C. HOMEWORK: WORD FORMS

Use the following chart to fill in the blanks with the correct word form. You may have to change verbs to past tense or nouns to plural. Use the correct form of the word for each number in the sentences below which have the same number. For example, use a correct form of *nation* in each of the sentences, 1.a. and 1.b.

	Noun	*Verb*	*Adjective*	*Adverb*
1.	nation	nationalize	national	nationally
2.	defense	defend	defensive	defensively
3.	control	control	(un)controllable	
4.	compliance	comply	compliant	compliantly
5.	competition	compete	competitive	competitively
6.	stability	stabilize	stable	
7.	inflation	inflate	inflated	
8.	balance	balance	balanced	
9.	expenditure	expend	expendable	
10.	interference	interfere	interfering	

1.a. Many of the ____________ of Europe belong to the Common Market.

b. Socialist governments usually ____________ large privately-owned industries.

2.a. The police rushed to the ____________ of their comrade when he was attacked by the street mob.

b. The owner of the factory spoke ____________ when the workers complained about their low wages.

3.a. Peoples of the world must learn to ____________ pollution.

b. Is the population explosion an ____________ problem?

4.a. The factory workers were reluctant to ____________ with the new no-smoking rule.

b. ____________ with the law is important to a stable society.

5.a. ____________ is important to a capitalist economy.

b. Young children usually ____________ for their parents' attention.

6.a. The government is trying to ____________ the economy by controlling inflation.

b. The ____________ of that new government is uncertain.

7.a. The high demand for sports cars quickly brought about ____________ prices.

b. An increase in salaries and wages will surely cause ____________.

8.a. The President tried to prepare a ____________ budget to send to Congress for approval.

b. A ____________ of work and relaxation is important in order to maintain physical and mental health.

9.a. The student ____________ a lot of energy on that assignment he did for his history class.

b. My monthly ____________ are over $800.

10.a. An ____________ mother-in-law can cause problems between a married couple.

b. Some economists believe that the government should never ____________ with the economy.

Follow-up: Check your answers with your teacher.

COMPREHENSIVE QUIZ DIRECTIONS

Now that you have completed from one to three chapters in this unit, your teacher may wish you to take a comprehensive quiz on the chapter or chapters which you have completed. Your teacher will tell you whether or not you can use your notes to answer the questions on this quiz. If you can use your notes, you should review them before taking the quiz so that you can anticipate the questions and know where to find the answers. If you cannot use your notes, *study them carefully before you take the quiz,* concentrating on organizing the information into main ideas and details which support these main ideas.

Before you begin writing your answers, read all the questions carefully. Your answers should be accurate and complete but brief. Do not include any information which does not answer the questions. You may have abbreviations in your notes, but do not use abbreviations in your answers. For those questions which are preceded by an asterisk, you must write your answers in complete sentences.

UNIT VI

Government and Law

Supreme Court decisions overturning state laws have led to marches on the steps of the court.

CHAPTER 16

Government by Constitution: Separation of Powers, Checks and Balances

1. Prelistening Activities

A. PREDICTIONS

Using the title of the lesson and the illustration as a starting point, share with your classmates what you already know or think about this topic. Then write three questions you think will be answered in this lecture.

1. ______________________________

2. ______________________________

3. ______________________________

Follow-up: After you have written your questions, share your questions with your teacher and your classmates.

B. VOCABULARY AND KEY CONCEPTS

Write the word or words you hear in the blanks provided in each sentence.

1. Two important principles of the United States Constitution are the ____________ of powers and the system of ____________ and ____________.

2. The Constitution provides for three ____________ of government: the ____________, the executive, and the ____________.

3. The legislative branch is primarily responsible for ____________, or making, new laws. The executive branch executes laws by signing them and by seeing that they are ____________.

4. The judicial branch deals with those who are ____________ ____________ ____________ a law or who are involved in a ____________ ____________.

5. The judicial branch also handles ____________ and reviews existing laws to make sure they are ____________ ____________ the U.S. Constitution.

6. Each branch has its specific ____________ and its own particular power, which it must not ____________.

7. The presidential ____________ ____________ ____________ is an obvious example of checks and balances.

8. Because it's difficult for Congress to ____________ a presidential veto, the veto may ____________ ____________ ____________ ____________ this new law forever.

9. Although President Nixon was ____________ of illegal activities, he was never removed from office by Congress because he ____________.

10. By finding laws against abortion ____________, the Supreme Court in effect made abortion ____________.

11. In the area of ____________ ____________, the Supreme Court declared it illegal to practice ____________ ____________ in any form.

12. Probably the most important effect of this change was the ____________ of public schools.

13. After the President ____________ ____________ ____________ for the Supreme Court, the Congress must ____________ his choice.

Follow-up: Check the spelling of the dictated words with your teacher. Discuss the meanings of these words and any other unfamiliar words in the sentences.

C. NOTETAKING SKILLS

Prelecture Reading

As we mentioned in the unit on education, U.S. university students most often prepare for each class by reading a text chapter, an article, or even a case study. This preparation makes the instructor's lecture, usually on a topic related to the reading, easier to follow and to take notes on.

Before listening to the lecture "Government by Constitution," read the following passage carefully and answer the comprehension questions. You will notice how this preparation will facilitate your comprehension of the lecture.

Judicial Review

Judicial review is the power of the courts to invalidate or overturn any law passed by the legislature which the court believes to be unconstitutional. The concept of judicial review as exercised by the Supreme Court of the United States is almost unique in the world. It can be called an American invention. Nowhere else does the judiciary of a country exercise final say over laws passed by the legislature. This enormous power of judicial review by the Supreme Court was established several years after the Constitution was written in a famous case, *Marbury* v. *Madison* (1803). In the Court's opinion it stated that the Constitution was superior to any acts by the legislature and that it was the Court's duty to void any laws which went against the Constitution. This power was not explicitly expressed in the Constitution, and even today, almost 200 years later, the Supreme Court's power to void laws passed by the legislature is still controversial.

If we compare judicial review in the United States with that in a few other countries, we will see just how unusual it is. In Great Britain, the right of Parliament (the legislature) to make any law it wants to cannot be challenged by the courts. The courts can *interpret* but not determine the validity of a law. In the Soviet Union there is no judicial review of legislature decisions made by the Supreme Soviet and the Presidium. Judicial review as exercised in the United States is viewed by the Soviets as being against the wishes of the majority and, as such, against democracy. In West Germany, the judiciary actually has had such power since shortly after World War II, but it has been slow to exercise this power for cultural and historical reasons. The judiciary in Canada has had this power on paper since 1982, but whether it will exercise it in a similar way to that exercised by the U.S. Supreme Court cannot be known yet.

Comprehension Questions

1. What is judicial review?

____

____

2. Is judicial review guaranteed by the United States Constitution? Explain.

___

___

3. Which of the following countries have no provisions for judicial review—Britain, the Soviet Union, Canada, West Germany?

___

___

4. Do West Germany and Canada exercise judicial review more or less frequently than the United States does? Explain.

___

___

Follow-up: Check your answers with your teacher before you continue.

2. Listening

A. FIRST LISTENING

The lecturer begins with a brief discussion of the Constitution of the United States and tells you its two guiding principles. She then announces her first subtopic, the three branches of the U.S. government. She goes on to explain these two principles. Finally, she expands on the second principle with several examples and illustrations. You will need to use the notetaking skills that you have learned to organize your notes on the blank notetaking page.

LECTURE

NOTES

Follow-up: How did you organize your notes? Yours may be different from another student's. What is important is that your notes reflect the basic organization and information of the lecture. If you don't feel confident about your notes, ask your teacher to show you an example of how a good set of notes could be organized.

B. SECOND (FINAL) LISTENING

Check the notes you have and fill in information you missed on the first listening.

LECTURE

Follow-up: Keeping in mind that you will use your notes later for a comprehensive quiz, check your notes with your teacher's or a classmate's.

3. Postlistening Activities

A. ACCURACY CHECK

Listen to the following statements. If the statement is true, put *T* in the space provided. If it is false, put *F*.

1. _____ 6. _____
2. _____ 7. _____
3. _____ 8. _____
4. _____ 9. _____
5. _____ 10. _____

Follow-up: Check your answers with your teacher. If you have less than 70% correct, you may need to listen to the lecture again. (If possible, try to make arrangements to listen again outside class.)

B. ORAL PRACTICE

B.1. Review: Your teacher will ask different students to use their notes to give different parts of the lecture to the whole class. For example, Student A will give the introduction, Student B will discuss the first major subtopic, and so on. The students who are listening should check the accuracy and completeness of their classmates' presentations.

Follow-up: Do you think your classmates left out any important information? If so, share your ideas with your class.

B.2. Transfer: Discuss with your class the following questions:

1. How is the power to make and enforce laws in your country divided? Explain.
2. Can a law be overturned by the judicial branch in your country? If so, under what circumstances?
3. Do you think the legislative branch of a government should have the power to remove the president of a country from office?

C. HOMEWORK: WORD FORMS

Use the following chart to fill in the blanks with the correct word form. You may have to change verbs to the past tense or nouns to plural. Use the correct form of the word for each number in the sentences below which have the same number. For example, use a correct form of *legality* in each of the sentences, 1.a. and 1.b.

	Noun	*Verb*	*Adjective*	*Adverb*
1.	legality	legalize	legal	legally
2.	abuse	abuse	abusive	abusively
3.	approval	approve	approving	approvingly
4.	suspicion suspect (person)	suspect	suspicious	suspiciously
5.	segregation	segregate	segregated	
6.	resignation	resign		

1.a. One cannot __________ take the property of another without permission.

b. Some people want to ____________ the use of marijuana and other drugs.

2.a. Some countries have laws which forbid the ____________ of children by parents.

b. The government used its power ____________ when it took the people's land.

3.a. I knew that I had done well on the work from the ____________ look my teacher gave me.

b. You will need the ____________ of your advisor before you can register for this course.

4.a. Nothing could ever make me ____________ you of bad intentions.

b. The poor man's free spending and luxurious purchases made the police ____________.

5.a. In some countries boys and girls are ____________ in school.

b. Public school ____________ was ended in the United States by a Supreme Court decision.

6.a. The president of the company was forced to ____________ when his crimes were discovered.

b. She would have ____________ her teaching position earlier, but she had many pressing debts.

Follow-up: Check your answers with your teacher.

bailiff—has custody of prisoners and maintains order in the court. **court clerk**—takes care of records involved in the court case. **court reporter**—keeps a written record of what is said in court. **judge**—sees that the trial is conducted according to the law. **witness**—a person who has knowledge of the case and is called to testify in court. **defendant**—the person against whom the court action has been taken. **the prosecutor/plaintiff**—the person who initiates court action against the plaintiff. **jury**—a body of persons who deliberate on the facts of the case and deliver a verdict (decision).

CHAPTER 17

Common Law and the Jury System

1. Prelistening Activities

A. PREDICTIONS

Using the title of the lesson and the illustration as a starting point, share with your classmates what you already know or think about this topic. Then write three questions you think will be answered in this lecture.

1. ____________________

2. ____________________

3. ____________________

Follow-up: After you have written your questions, share your questions with your teacher and your classmates.

B. VOCABULARY AND KEY CONCEPTS

Write the word or words you hear in the blanks provided in each sentence.

1. The average person in the legal profession would probably say it's better to let a dozen ____________ people go free than to punish one innocent person ____________ .

2. The guiding principle for the U.S. legal system is that an accused person is __________ __________ __________ __________.

3. Under civil law the judge consults a complex __________ __________ __________ to decide whether the defendant is guilty and, if so, what sentence to give.

4. Under __________ __________ the judge considers the __________ set by other court decisions.

5. The jury's responsibility is to hear __________ in either civil or criminal trials and reach a __________.

6. The judge guides the jurors by deciding what evidence is allowed and by __________ __________ __________ by lawyers and witnesses.

7. If the required number of jurors don't agree on a verdict, it is a __________ __________, and the law requires a new __________.

8. What happens in plea bargaining is that the accused __________ __________ to a __________ __________.

Follow-up: Check the spelling of the dictated words with your teacher. Discuss the meanings of these words and any other unfamiliar words in the sentences.

C. NOTETAKING SKILLS

Prelecture Reading

Before listening to a rather difficult lecture on the U.S. legal system, read a related passage dealing with *precedents* and surrogate motherhood and answer the comprehension questions which follow. Although somewhat difficult, the reading and the questions will prepare you to understand better the lecture you will listen to later.

The Baby M Case

The Baby M case became a controversial legal case in the United States in 1988. What was at issue were Baby M's custody and the validity of a contract. The contract provided that a woman, the surrogate mother, would have a baby for an infertile couple by artificial insemination of the husband's sperm and would receive payment for this service. Certainly Baby M was not the first baby born to a surrogate mother, but in this case the surrogate mother, Mary Beth Whitehead-Gould, changed her mind after the baby was born and did not want to give the baby up as she had agreed to do in the contract. The Sterns, the couple who had contracted for the baby, insisted that Ms. Whitehead-Gould fulfill the terms of the contract, and they took her to court. The New Jersey Supreme Court ruled that this type of contract was against public policy (the good of the general public) and, therefore, could not be enforced. (However, the court did award *custody* of the baby to the father. The mother, Ms. Whitehead-Gould, was awarded limited visitation rights.) This particular ruling was very important because there had been no previous court decision of this type at the level of a state supreme court before. Therefore, this decision establishes a precedent for other states when they have to deal with this issue of surrogacy.

Comprehension Questions

1. Are Baby M's natural mother and father married to each other?

   ____

   ____

2. Who wanted to break the contract, Mary Beth Whitehead-Gould or the Sterns?

____

____

3. In this reading, "precedent" most nearly means
   a. a reason not to do something
   b. a decision used as a standard
   c. proof of innocence
   d. proof of guilt

4. Was there a precedent for judging surrogacy contracts before the Baby M case?

____

____

5. In what sense will the Baby M case serve as a precedent in the future?

____

____

Follow-up: Discuss your answers with your teacher before you continue.

2. Listening

A. FIRST LISTENING

The lecturer begins with a rather long introduction in which the lecturer is attempting to provide some background to a rather technical discussion of the U.S. legal system which is based on common law. She then goes on to discuss the jury system and, finally, plea bargaining. It is not necessary to take notes until she begins to compare common law to civil law. Use the notetaking skills you have practiced to make a set of meaningful and usable notes.

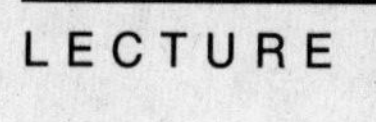

NOTES

Follow-up: How did you organize your notes? Your notes may be different from another student's. What is important is that your notes should reflect the basic organization and information of the lecture. (Check to see if your prediction questions were answered.)

B. SECOND (FINAL) LISTENING

Check the notes you have and fill in the information you missed on the first listening.

LECTURE

Follow-up: Keeping in mind that you will use your notes later for a comprehensive quiz, check your notes with your teacher's, or a classmate's.

3. Postlistening Activities

A. ACCURACY CHECK

Listen to the following statements. If the statement is true, put *T* in the space provided. If it is false, put *F*.

1.	______	6.	______
2.	______	7.	______
3.	______	8.	______
4.	______	9.	______
5.	______	10.	______

Follow-up: Check your answers with your teacher. If you had less than 70% correct, you may need to listen to the lecture again and check the accuracy and completeness of your notes. (If possible, try to make arrangements to listen again outside class.)

B. ORAL PRACTICE

B.1. Review: Your teacher will ask different students to use their notes to give different parts of the lecture to the whole class. Student A will compare common and civil law. Student B will discuss the jury system in the United States, and Student C will discuss plea bargaining. The students who are listening should check the accuracy and completeness of their classmates' presentations.

Follow-up: Do you think your classmates left out any important information? If so, share your ideas with your class.

B.2. Transfer: Discuss the following questions with a classmate or as a class:

1. If you were on trial for a crime, would you rather have a jury decide your guilt or innocence or would you prefer to have a judge make that decision? Explain.
2. Should plea bargaining ever be allowed in a legal system? If so, under what circumstances? If not, why not?

C. HOMEWORK: READING COMPREHENSION

Read the passage in order to answer the questions which follow.

National and Tribal Law

Our lecture on the U.S. legal system might mistakenly give the impression that common law and civil law are the only two kinds of law in the world. Although common and civil law are very widespread, they are by no means the only kinds of law. Many countries have national and tribal laws which have developed with a unique character of their own, which reflects the history and predominant religion of the countries. Both China and Japan are examples of countries with traditional national laws. Western influence does, however, show up in the laws of these countries today.

There is a general tendency for countries with their own unique systems of laws to "westernize" the systems. The negative side of the westernization is, of course, the loss of national traditions; the positive side is the possibility of closer international cooperation where laws, especially those governing business and commerce, are similar.

Another system of law which developed quite independently of western influences was Islamic law, *shari'ah*. Today, Islamic law is not followed to the same degree in all Muslim countries, however. Turkey, for example, follows European legal codes exclusively, while Saudi Arabia follows the *shari'ah* very closely. Other Muslim countries such as Pakistan, Egypt, and Muslim African countries compromise by using western law for many civil and criminal matters while following Islamic law for all matters related to marriage, divorce, and inheritance.

Comprehension Questions

1. What exactly are national and tribal laws?

   ____

   ____

2. Why is it helpful for different countries to have similar laws concerning business and commerce?

   ____

   ____

3. In countries with national laws, why do you suppose laws concerning business have often changed while those governing family matters have not?

   ____

   ____

4. In your opinion is there a movement in the world toward world culture, that is, an internationalization of certain aspects of culture?

   ____

   ____

Follow-up: Check your answers with your teacher.

CHAPTER 18

The Political Process: The Two-Party System*

1. Prelistening Activities

A. PREDICTIONS

Using the title of the lesson and the illustration as a starting point, share with your classmates what you already know or think about this topic. Then write three questions you think will be answered in this lecture.

1. ______________________________

2. ______________________________

3. ______________________________

Follow-up: After you have written your questions, share your questions with your teacher and your classmates.

*It may be helpful to do the homework reading for this lesson as a prelecture reading instead of as homework

B. VOCABULARY AND KEY CONCEPTS

Write the word or words you hear in the blanks provided in each sentence.

1. The United States is a democracy, which means that citizens elect their leaders and ____________ all the way from the local and state level to the national level.

2. Conservatives in the United States believe that the purpose of government is to provide protection for people and to ____________ their freedom to conduct their own lives as they ____________ ____________.

3. Conservatives are less likely to want to change the ____________ ____________ while liberals are more apt to want to make ____________ social changes.

4. There is a price to be paid for not ____________ oneself with either major party.

5. There is quite a lot of ____________ between the two parties, with some Republicans calling themselves "progressive" and many Democrats who are quite conservative on many issues.

6. Republicans tend to be more ____________, older, white middle- and upper-class voters.

7. A President of one party is often able to work with a Congress with a majority of members of the ____________ party.

8. One strength of the two-party system is that it can elect a President of one party and send a majority of a different party to Congress without ____________ the government.

9. The two-party system is able to ____________ a wide variety of ____________ without encouraging a lot of small factions.

10. The two-party system forces a lot of ____________ within a party and helps to ____________ political parties.

11. The two-party system makes it possible for Republicans and Democrats to cooperate in Congress and with the President on some issues where ____________ support is necessary.

12. The two-party system has allowed for a large degree of political ____________ and ____________ throughout some fairly turbulent times in spite of its faults and ____________.

Follow-up: Check the spelling of the dictated words with your teacher. Discuss the meanings of these words and any other unfamiliar words in the sentences.

C. NOTETAKING SKILLS

Qualifying Statements

The lecturer's topic today, the two-party system in the United States, by its nature forces the lecturer to *qualify* many of the statements. Qualifying words are words such as *many, most, few, some, all, always, sometimes, usually, in general, generally speaking,* etc. Qualifying words are very important to pay attention to in order to avoid *overgeneralizing.* The lecturer has to generalize somewhat when discussing this topic but tries to be very careful to remind you that she *is* generalizing. In this lecture you will hear the following qualifying words and phrases:

in a general way
in very general terms
likely, less likely, more likely, unlikely
very generally

many exceptions
very broadly speaking
for the most part
on the whole
usually
most
tend to
apt to

If you are unfamiliar with the meaning of any of these words or phrases, you should discuss them with your teacher or check them in a dictionary. Then pay attention to these words as you listen to the lecture about the two-party system in the United States.

Rhetorical Cues

While the lecturer has a plan for, or organization to, the lecture, from time to time she digresses from the topic for a short time and discusses an offshoot of the topic. In this lecture these offshoots are fairly closely related to the topic, but strictly speaking are somewhat off the topic. For example, the lecturer has said that she will discuss reasons that people support one or the other of the two major parties. Then during the discussion, she decides to mention that it is not necessary to support either of these two parties and goes on to discuss other smaller parties and the implications of supporting one of these parties. The lecturer goes somewhat off-topic three times during the lecture and introduces these off-topic remarks, as follows:

I probably should point out here . . .
I should also tell you . . .
By the way, I probably should point out to you . . .

It's difficult to know when a lecturer goes off the topic whether or not you need to take notes on what the lecturer says. In this case, since the lecturer uses the word "should" in the introduction to these remarks, what she has to say probably seems important to her, and you should try to take notes on what she says.

As you get more experienced taking notes in the "real world" of university classes, you will notice more and more that lecturers frequently go off the topic. "By the way" is a favorite way of many lecturers to announce that they are about to go off the topic. These off-topic remarks often consist of a personal experience, a joke, and even occasionally a little gossip. A lecturer's body language and facial expression will often change as he or she goes off the topic and will change again as he or she returns to the topic. Experienced notetakers notice these changes and know when they can relax a little and when they need to get back to serious notetaking.

Follow-up: Did you already know the words and expressions that indicate that a person is generalizing? If not, did you discuss them with your teacher or look them up in a dictionary? If so, you are ready to listen to the lecture.

2. Listening

A. FIRST LISTENING

The lecturer begins by noting the kind of political system the United States has, calling your attention particularly to the two-party system. The lecturer goes on to discuss the two major political parties in some detail, reasons people have for supporting one or the other party, the kind of people likely to be in each party, and concludes with the strengths of the two-party system. You will need to use the notetaking skills that you have learned to organize your notes on the blank notetaking page.

LECTURE

NOTES

Follow-up: Let's review a few notetaking skills. Were you able to *structure* your notes, determine *relevant* information, write down *key words, abbreviate* whenever possible, and use *rhetorical cues?* In other words, were you able to use most or all the relevant notetaking skills you have previously practiced?

B. SECOND (FINAL) LISTENING

Check the notes you have and fill in information you missed on the first listening.

LECTURE

Follow-up: Keeping in mind that you will use your notes later for a comprehensive quiz, check your notes with your teacher's or a classmate's.

3. Postlistening Activities

A. ACCURACY CHECK

Listen to the following statements. If the statement is true, put *T* in the space provided. If it is false, put *F*.

1. ______ 6. ______
2. ______ 7. ______
3. ______ 8. ______
4. ______ 9. ______
5. ______ 10. ______

Follow-up: Check your answers with your teacher. If you have less than 70% correct, you may need to listen to the lecture again. (If possible, try to make arrangements to listen again outside class.)

B. ORAL PRACTICE

B.1. Review: Your teacher will ask different students to use their notes to give different parts of the lecture to the whole class. For example, Student A will give the introduction, Student B will discuss the first major subtopic, and so on. The students who are listening should check the accuracy and completeness of their classmates' presentations.

Follow-up: Do you think your classmates left out any important information? If so, share your ideas with your class.

B.2. Transfer: Discuss with your class the following questions:

1. Do you have political parties in your country? If so, how is the party system different from that in the United States?
2. The lecturer told you about some of the strengths of the two-party system. What do you think some of the weaknesses are?
3. What other kinds of systems for choosing national leaders are you familiar with?

C. HOMEWORK: READING COMPREHENSION

Read the following and answer the comprehension questions.

The Presidential and the Vice-Presidential Election Process

The President and the Vice President are the only two *nationally* elected officials of the United States, and the process involved in selecting candidates to run for these offices and the process by which the President and the Vice President are ultimately chosen are fairly complex.

Months before the election itself, which is held every four years in November, many individual states begin to hold *primaries,* statewide elections in which each party selects delegates committed to certain candidates to send to the national convention of each party, both of which are held in the summer months. The number of delegates a state sends is determined by the size of the population of that state. Some state delegates are chosen at local party *caucuses,* which are meetings open to members of the party, but most delegates are chosen by statewide primary elections, in which much larger numbers of people can, of course, participate.

Often many hopeful presidential candidates will compete for delegates in these primaries from state to state for as long as their supporters feel they have any chance to win the support of a large number of delegates. The first few primaries are considered very important in testing a candidate's credibility and viability as a presidential candidate. Every word and action of the candidate will be carefully reported, and any weakness he or she shows will be exploited by the media. This can be a very tough, sometimes cruel, time for candidates, as one careless word or action can be disastrous, but some people feel it is very useful in weeding out candidates who are unsuitable to be President for any reason. Other people feel just as strongly that good people can be destroyed by this intense media scrutiny.

At any rate, when the time comes, the delegates will go to the national convention held by each party and cast their ballots for the candidate they are committed to. Although neither party currently has a rule *requiring* delegates to vote for a particular candidate, nor does the Constitution require this, most delegates will vote for the candidate that the voters of their state indicated as their choice, at least for the first ballot. There are some uncommitted delegates, however, who might become very important in the case that no candidate has a majority of delegates committed to him or her before the first ballot. If one candidate receives over 50% of the votes of the delegates on the first ballot, that is the end of the story. However, if no candidate receives 50% of the votes on the first ballot, there will begin a process of bargaining and power brokering of delegate votes during subsequent ballots. This gives a candidate who has less than 50% of the delegates committed to him or her a chance to win over some more delegates and possibly to win the nomination* itself or at least a chance to use those delegates committed to him or her to bargain for political power inside the party and a chance to influence other candidates.

At any rate, each party will eventually choose its candidate in the rather carnival-like atmosphere of its national convention. The presidential candidate will then choose his or her vice-presidential running mate. This choice is also influenced by political considerations, particularly a desire to balance the ticket. This means that the presidential candidate will try to choose a running mate from a different part of the country—for example, to appeal to voters from that area—and even choose a running mate with somewhat different political leanings. For example, a rather liberal Democrat

*nomination: from *to nominate*, or to appoint as a candidate for an office. A nomination often comes at the conclusion of a nominating speech. The nominated person is called the nominee.

may choose a somewhat more conservative Democratic running mate to reassure conservative Democrats and convince them to vote for a Democratic and not a Republican candidate. Now begins the final few months of campaigning.

The final months of campaigning are very intense and very expensive. Candidates will keep up grueling speaking schedules and make as many public appearances in front of as many groups as possible. A lot of money will be spent on advertising, particularly TV advertising. Issues will be discussed, but often superficially, as candidates try to appeal to the greatest number of people in both parties as possible. At this point campaigns can become rather "rough and tumble" as each side tries to win voters and to discredit the other side. Accusations and counteraccusations become increasingly emotional and personal.

Because of a system called "winner-take-all," which means that a candidate who receives more than 50% of the popular votes in a state will win the whole state, candidates will concentrate their efforts on those states with the largest population they think they have a reasonable chance of winning or on states they feel they must win if they are to have any chance to win the election. States with large populations such as California, New York, and Illinois will usually be "hotly contested." Candidates will, for all intents and purposes, "write off" certain states they believe to be unwinnable or that have small numbers of voters. Finally, on election day the voters will go to the polls and vote for the candidate and his or her running mate of their choice.

One final oddity about the U.S. presidential election process: Voters do not vote directly for the candidate of their choice. They actually vote for electors, or members of the electoral college. These are state representatives of the party who will cast ballots for the presidential candidate several weeks after the election. Because of the "winner-take-all" system, it is technically possible for a candidate to win a greater number of electors without winning a majority of the popular vote. There is talk from time to time of changing this system and making this important election one based solely on the popular vote. However, for complicated political reasons this is not likely to happen anytime soon.

1. How often and when is a presidential election held?

____

____

2. What is the purpose of the state primary elections?

____

____

3. What is a party caucus? How is it different from a primary?

____

____

4. Why are the first few primaries considered to be especially important?

____

____

5. Why do some people criticize primaries?

____

____

6. It is possible to know who will be the candidate of a particular party before the national convention is held? Explain your answer.

____

____

7. What are some of the criteria a presidential nominee might use in selecting his or her vice-presidential running mate?

____

____

8. What does "winner-take-all" mean, and how does it affect the way candidates campaign?

____

____

____

____

9. Why are campaign issues often discussed only superficially during the presidential campaign?

____

____

10. Is it possible for a candidate to receive fewer popular votes and still win the presidency? Explain your answer.

____

____

Follow-up: Check your answers with your teacher.

COMPREHENSIVE QUIZ DIRECTIONS

Now that you have completed from one to three chapters in this unit, your teacher may wish you to take a comprehensive quiz on the chapter or chapters which you have completed. Your teacher will tell you whether or not you can use your notes to answer the questions on this quiz. If you can use your notes, you should review them before taking the quiz so that you can anticipate the questions and know where to find the answers. If you cannot use your notes, *study them carefully before you take the quiz,* concentrating on organizing the information into main ideas and details which support these main ideas.

Before you begin writing your answers, read all the questions carefully. Your answers should be accurate and complete but brief. Do not include any information which does not answer the questions. You may have abbreviations in your notes, but do not use abbreviations in your answers. For those questions which are preceded by an asterisk, you must write your answers in complete sentences.

Comprehensive Quiz: Unit I

CHAPTER 1. POPULATION

1. What does the U.S. population consist of in terms of race and origin? (Use percentages.)

____

____

2. List the five Eastern states which are among the United States' most populous states.

____

____

3. List the remaining five most populous states, which are located in the West, the Midwest, and the South-Central United States. (Write the states under the name of the area in which they are found.)

The West *The Midwest* *The South-Central States*

*4. Discuss the ratio of men to women in the U.S. population. (Mention the proportion of men to women as well as birth and death rates for men and women.)

____

____

____

____

5. Give the average age of the U.S population and tell whether it's increasing or decreasing.

____

____

CHAPTER 2. FOREIGN STUDENT POPULATION

*1. Compare the average yearly increase in foreign students studying in the United States in the last half of the 1970s to the increase between the academic years 1984/85 and 1985/86.

2. List the areas that most foreign students in the United States in 1985/86 came from. List them in order of the area sending the most students to the area sending the fewest.

*3. Compare the total foreign student population in the United States to the numbers coming from South and East Asia and from the Middle East in the academic year 1985/86.

4. List the three biggest fields of interest, or majors, of foreign students in the United States and the percentages of students enrolled in each field.

*5. Compare the number of foreign undergraduate students to the number of foreign graduate students for the academic year 1985/86.

CHAPTER 3. IMMIGRATION: PAST AND PRESENT

*1. At the time of independence in 1776, what was the ethnic composition of the population which had immigrated to or settled in what is now the United States? Why was the country primarily British in tradition and language?

____

____

____

____

____

____

2. List the numbers and countries of origin of immigrants to the United States during the following stages of the Great Immigration.

1830–1860:

____

____

1860–1890:

____

____

1890–1930:

____

____

3. List at least four specific reasons that Europeans immigrated to the United States between 1830 and 1930.

____

____

____

____

CHAPTER 3. IMMIGRATION: PAST AND PRESENT

*4. After 1930, how did U.S. laws and world events contribute to the decline in immigration to the United States?

____

____

____

____

____

____

5. What countries do most recent immigrants come from?

____

____

*6. How are the immigrants coming to the United States today different from those who came during the Great Immigration? (Consider their reasons for coming, where they come from, the U.S. government's policies towards them, and how the United States is different today from the time of the Great Immigration.)

____

____

____

____

____

____

____

____

Comprehensive Quiz: Unit II

CHAPTER 4. GEOGRAPHY

1. What is the area of the United States in square miles?

____

____

2. How long are the U.S. borders with both Canada and Mexico?

____

____

3. What fractions of the total U.S. area do the Intermontane Plateau and interior lowland make up?

Plateau: __________

Lowland: __________

*4. Discuss the location and elevation of the three major U.S. mountain ranges.

____

____

____

____

____

____

*5. Explain why the Mississippi is the most important river in the United States.

____

____

CHAPTER 4. GEOGRAPHY

***Bonus Question:** The Great Lakes are important to the economy of the United States. Explain why you think this is true.

___

___

___

___

CHAPTER 5. CLIMATE

1. How many climate types are there in the world, and how many of these are found in the United States?

*2. Compare the rates of precipitation in the East to those in the West. Give the ranges of precipitation rates (from . . . inches to . . . inches) and tell which region is wetter.

3. Describe the probable weather of these two eastern cities in summer and winter:

Bangor, Maine
(an interior northern city)

Atlanta, Georgia
(a southern city)

*4. Why does the western half of the United States have a generally drier climate than the eastern half?

CHAPTER 5. CLIMATE

*5. Explain why latitude is not as important an influence on climate in the West as it is in the East.

CHAPTER 6. AGRICULTURE

1. Give three reasons for the United States' high agricultural productivity.

____

____

*2. Put the following groups in order in terms of their importance in U.S. agriculture. Put the number 1 by the most important and the number 4 by the least important.

_____ fruits and vegetables

_____ livestock and dairy products

_____ grains

_____ nonedible products (cotton, tobacco)

*3. Which region of the United States is the most important in terms of agricultural production: the West, the North, the middle part of the United States (which includes the Midwest), or the South? Give examples of production to support your answer.

____

____

____

____

4. List three ways that technology is used in agriculture in the United States.

____

____

*5. Explain why most U.S. farmers are not very rich people.

____

____

Comprehensive Quiz: Unit III

CHAPTER 7. THE NUCLEAR FAMILY

*1. Explain the difference between a nuclear and an extended family.

____

____

____

____

____

____

*2. Why are there so many single-parent families in the United States, and what is their economic situation in general?

____

____

____

____

____

____

*3. Discuss the historical reasons for the prevalence of the nuclear family in the United States.

____

____

____

____

____

____

____

____

CHAPTER 7. THE NUCLEAR FAMILY

*4. Discuss the economic reasons which have influenced the development of the nuclear family.

*5. How do American children show their independence?

CHAPTER 8. RELIGION

*1. Why are there so many different religious groups in the United States?

____

____

____

____

2. Name two practices that are not allowed due to separation of church and state.

____

____

*3. Is separation of church and state *absolute*? Explain your answer.

____

____

____

____

*4. Explain how churches are important in the social lives of many Americans.

____

____

____

____

CHAPTER 9. PASSAGES: BIRTH, MARRIAGE, AND DEATH

1. Describe a *baby shower* in as much detail as you can.

*2. Describe a change in the role of some modern American fathers at the birth of a baby.

3. Who traditionally pays for a wedding?

*4. Describe two customs surrounding a wedding which are rather superstitious in nature.

CHAPTER 9. PASSAGES: BIRTH, MARRIAGE, AND DEATH

5. What are three decisions that must be made at the time of death?

*6. What kind of card can you send to the family of a person who has died? What kind of flowers should you send to a funeral?

Comprehensive Quiz: Unit IV

CHAPTER 10. PUBLIC EDUCATION: PHILOSOPHY AND FUNDING

1. What are the two features of the American educational system that are different from those in most other countries?

*2. Compare the different responsibilities of the state department of education, the local school district, and the local school itself.

3. What is an *elective*?

4. How are people on a local school board chosen?

CHAPTER 10. PUBLIC EDUCATION: PHILOSOPHY AND FUNDING

5. Where does the money to fund U.S. schools come from? (Give percentages.)

*6. Explain how the U.S. system of funding schools results in an educational inequity.

CHAPTER 11. POSTSECONDARY EDUCATION: ADMISSIONS

1. Approximately how many accredited U.S. colleges and universities are there in the United States?

2. Describe the range in numbers of students a college or university may have and the range in yearly cost.

3. Where are these colleges and universities located?

4. What two things do most colleges and universities ask a student to submit along with his application?

*5. Discuss factors colleges and universities consider besides test scores and grades *and why*?

*6. The lecturer discusses the situation at one southwestern state university. He uses the figures 20%, 1/3, and 60% in talking about high school students who enter this school as freshmen. What do these figures refer to?

CHAPTER 11. POSTSECONDARY EDUCATION: ADMISSIONS

*7. Discuss how junior colleges differ from four-year colleges and universities.

CHAPTER 12. UNIVERSITY LIFE

*1. Discuss the possible diversity of the student body at an American college or university.

*2. Discuss the reasons that the lecturer suggests for why foreign students often find American college students to be poorly prepared.

*3. Describe a typical American college professor and his expectations for the students in his class.

*4. Write a paragraph describing what a good syllabus will include.

CHAPTER 12. UNIVERSITY LIFE

*5. Write a paragraph describing how graduate school is different from undergraduate school.

Comprehensive Quiz: Unit V

CHAPTER 13. THE ECONOMY AT HOME AND IN THE WORLD

1. What two factors explain why the United States is such a great economic power?

____

____

2. Define these two terms:

   a. gross national product

   ____

   ____

   b. negative balance of trade

   ____

   ____

3. How is the labor force in the United States divided, that is, what are the sectors and percentages (approximate) of people in each one?

____

____

____

____

*4. What is the service sector and how has it changed in this century?

____

____

____

____

____

____

CHAPTER 13. THE ECONOMY AT HOME AND IN THE WORLD

5. Who are the United States' major trading partners?

6. a. What are the United States' major exports?

   b. What are the United States' major imports?

*7. Explain why the U.S. economy has such a big impact on other countries although the U.S. labor force comprises only 6% of the world labor force.

CHAPTER 14. CAPITALISM U.S. STYLE

*1. Describe in as much detail as possible the differences between a socialist economy and a capitalist economy.

2. Which two countries are closer to the pure socialist model and which two countries are closer to the pure capitalist model?

*3. Write how business decisions are made in a market economy in as much detail as you can.

*4. Define or explain *supply and demand.*

CHAPTER 14. CAPITALISM U.S. STYLE

5. What are the three characteristics of U.S. capitalism?

*6. Choose *one* of the three characteristics of U.S. capitalism and explain it in as much detail as you can.

CHAPTER 15. THE ROLE OF GOVERNMENT IN THE ECONOMY

*1. In a pure capitalist economy, what would the government's responsibilities be limited to?

2. Define the following terms:
   a. public assistance

   b. antitrust or monopoly laws

   c. government expenditures

   d. taxation

3. What are the four reasons that the government tries to regulate the economy?

CHAPTER 15. THE ROLE OF GOVERNMENT IN THE ECONOMY

*4. Describe how the government tries to maintain economic stability in terms of taxation, expenditure, and interest rates.

Comprehensive Quiz: Unit VI

CHAPTER 16. GOVERNMENT BY CONSTITUTION: SEPARATION OF POWERS, CHECKS AND BALANCES

1. Mention the three branches of government and state briefly what each does.

____

____

____

____

*2. In one sentence, define *separation of powers.*

____

____

3. Why does the United States Constitution provide a system of checks and balances?

____

____

*4. Give an example of how the executive branch can check the legislative branch and another example of how the legislative branch can check the executive branch.

____

____

____

____

5. In the lecture, what were the examples of abortion and civil rights used to illustrate?

____

____

CHAPTER 16. GOVERNMENT BY CONSTITUTION: SEPARATION OF POWERS, CHECKS AND BALANCES

*6. Is there any check on the power of the Supreme Court? Explain.

CHAPTER 17. COMMON LAW AND THE JURY SYSTEM

*1. Discuss the major differences between common law and civil law.

____

____

____

____

2. What does a jury decide in each of these two cases:

   a. a civil lawsuit?

   ____

   ____

   b. a criminal case?

   ____

   ____

*3. Explain (a) what is meant by a *hung jury* and (b) what is required by law when a hung jury occurs.

____

____

*4. How does the legal system try to make sure that a jury does not contain people who are insane or prejudiced?

____

____

____

____

5. Explain why plea bargaining is often agreed to by

   a. the state/the prosecutor

   ____

   ____

b. the accused

____

____

CHAPTER 18. THE POLITICAL PROCESS: THE TWO-PARTY SYSTEM

*1. Describe the difference in beliefs and ideas between conservatives and liberals in the United States in general terms. Include only main ideas.

____

____

____

____

____

____

____

____

____

____

*2. In a sentence explain why the southern states are more likely to vote Democrat. Be specific.

____

____

3. Which party, the Republican or Democratic, would be more *likely* to support the following?

a. a woman's right to an abortion

____

b. increased military spending

____

c. the interests of big business

____

d. lower taxes

____

CHAPTER 18. THE POLITICAL PROCESS: THE TWO-PARTY SYSTEM

e. strong antipollution laws

____

f. a law requiring businesses to hire minorities

____

g. federal financial aid to university students

____

*4. Explain why the greatest number of people support one or the other of the two major parties even though they may not agree with all the policies of the party of their choice.

____

____

____

____

*5. Explain what the lecturer means when he says there is a lot of *overlap* between the Democratic and Republican parties.

____

____

____

____

6. List the advantages of the two-party system as it works in the United States.

____

____

____

____